Style & Substance

Style
&
Substance

A GUIDE TO FINDING
AND JOINING THE
ACADEMIC CONVERSATION

John
Lambersky

broadview press

BROADVIEW PRESS — www.broadviewpress.com
Peterborough, Ontario, Canada

Founded in 1985, Broadview Press remains a wholly independent publishing house. Broadview's focus is on academic publishing; our titles are accessible to university and college students as well as scholars and general readers. With over 800 titles in print, Broadview has become a leading international publisher in the humanities, with world-wide distribution. Broadview is committed to environmentally responsible publishing and fair business practices.

Library and Archives Canada Cataloguing in Publication

Title: Style & substance : a guide to finding and joining the academic conversation / John
    Lambersky.
Other titles: Style and substance
Names: Lambersky, John, author.
Description: Includes bibliographical references and index.
Identifiers: Canadiana (print) 20220400970 | Canadiana (ebook) 20220401055 | ISBN
    9781554815906 (softcover) | ISBN 9781770488656 (PDF) | ISBN 9781460408018 (EPUB)
Subjects: LCSH: Academic writing. | LCSH: English language—Rhetoric.
Classification: LCC PE1478 .L36 2022 | DDC 808/.042—dc23

Broadview Press handles its own distribution in North America:
PO Box 1243, Peterborough, Ontario K9J 7H5, Canada
555 Riverwalk Parkway, Tonawanda, NY 14150, USA
Tel: (705) 743-8990; Fax: (705) 743-8353
email: customerservice@broadviewpress.com

For all territories outside of North America, distribution is handled by Eurospan Group.

Broadview Press acknowledges the financial support of the Government of Canada for our publishing activities.

Edited by Tania Therien
Book design by Michel Vrana

PRINTED IN CANADA

This little book is written in the hope that it will explain and demystify the skills required to be the best researcher, writer, presenter, and defender of ideas you can possibly be.

May finding and joining the academic conversation be a lifelong journey.

Contents

This Whole Book Shrunk to Fit on Two Pages

The Short List

The list below is the shortest of shortcuts to what comes afterward. The rest of the book is dedicated to explaining the why and how—but if you get lost, return to this list.

Learn

1. Before you write, learn what others have said. All writing is part of a conversation that is already going on.
2. Always allow your ideas to be shaped by research. Never have your research dictated by your ideas.

Plan

3. Once you have learned a little about this conversation, decide what you wish to say, what is worth saying, and whose voices in that conversation you will highlight. Not all voices are equally worthwhile.
4. Put that intention into a plan—call it an outline if you want—and follow that outline when it makes sense, but know you can and should go off the path if need be.

Write

5. Write, but don't feel the need to start at the beginning, or write each sentence in order, from the start to the end.

Introductions are often best written once the main part of the piece has been drafted.

6. Consider alternative explanations and other views in your writing. This doesn't undermine your writing: it strengthens it. Make those other views explicitly clear. Put various voices in conversation.

Revise

7. Revise your writing carefully, word by word and sentence by sentence. In time spent, the ratio of revision to fresh writing should ideally be at least 3:1. (In your best pieces, it's likely to be more like 5:1.)

8. When revising, remember that writing is part art and part science; the science part dictates rules of composition that even the best writer can't ignore. Readers' brains are more alike than different.

9. Your writing needs to be as nearly perfect as possible. Don't be seduced by "that should be good enough." A collection of even small errors in style, gaps in reasoning, or missing sources threatens the value of your work.

Extend

10. Keep adding your voice to the ongoing story of ideas. Your work on any topic is never really done; keep reading, keep writing, keep speaking. (And remember: as you read, so shall you write.)

... And return to step one above as often as possible.

CHAPTER 1

Join the Academic Conversation with Grace

"Is There Really a Better Way to Write?"

SEEN CORRECTLY, WRITING IS NOTHING MORE AND NOTHING less than communication between you and a reader. It is intimate: reading is often done quietly, while alone; the reader has no access to anything but what you share with them; you and the reader have, if even just briefly, a kind of relationship. And in that relationship, you are the leader. You select the words that convey your meaning, arrange them artfully, and hope that in doing so, you are able to achieve something in the mind of the reader. Writing is about meeting the needs of another person.

An awareness of those needs should be kept close to you as you write. And beneath those needs is a complex story. Pause a moment and notice what is happening as someone reads. At the microscopic level, the act of reading is quite staggering. A person looks at symbols on a page—we call them letters—and inside their brain, those symbols are strung together to form words, which connect in all sorts of meaningful ways to actual, lived things. Three simple letters, "c-a-r," immediately bring to mind a ton of steel, glass, and plastic, notions of teenage freedom, the romance of the open road, the smell of a new vehicle fresh from the dealership, and a thousand other things besides. When reading, the electrical and chemical signals of our brains are a flurry—even when imagining something as simple as a car.[1] When words are used carefully, to communicate rich and thoughtful ideas, the magnitude of the achievement is all the more great. Consider these lines from the US Declaration of Independence: "We hold these truths to be self-evident, that all men are created equal, that they are endowed by their Creator with certain unalienable Rights, that among these are Life, Liberty and the pursuit of Happiness." Contained in that one sentence is a constellation of ideas about how human beings should organize themselves in society and about what it means to be a human. Not long before Thomas Jefferson wrote those words, it was seen as self-evident that the few should rule over the many, and that those kings and lords could rule in ways indifferent to the quality of life under them. It is not an exaggeration to say that these words inspired millions of people to fight for a different kind of existence.[2] After reading these kinds of words, the minds of readers contained ideas that did not exist before, demands that had previously not had a shape—these words willed into existence new ways of organizing human life. Without these words, and words like them, how could we have ever

---

1   See for example Baretta et al. for an interesting study on the use of electroencephalography (EEG) devices to measure brain activity while reading.

2   Indeed, as many have pointed out, women and people of color were excluded from early American conceptions of rights and freedoms, and this document, along with others, inspired many of the rights movements that would follow to shape the world into a more humane place.

hoped for human rights and responsible government? All this from curiously shaped symbols on a page we call letters. Letters shaped words, words shaped brains, and the world changed.

The act of reading is so common now, and its fruits so widely distributed, that we take for granted the secular miracle that is literacy. In fortunate nations like ours, nearly everyone has learned to read and write—at least, to some degree. Our blessing of literacy has been the culmination of at least a few centuries' hard work and society-wide megaprojects like mandatory schooling. If you are anything like me and like most people, you are likely less than three human lifetimes away from illiteracy. In 1800, according to data from the Organisation for Economic Co-Operation and Development (OECD) and UNESCO, only around 12 per cent of the world population was literate (Roser and Ortiz-Ospina). Your ancestors had words, and might have been gifted at using them, but those words were temporary. They were conversations; they existed alongside almost always only hand gestures, helpful back-and-forths to clarify meaning when needed, and the gift of eye contact. The Earth is very old, we are very young, and writing is very new indeed. We haven't been doing it for very long, and while language might come naturally to us, no one is born able to write.

You would be forgiven for thinking that each of us writes in our own way, and that this is a good thing. Superficially, this writing-as-individual style idea has truth to it; no two people will write *exactly* the same way. We each bring our own background experiences, personalities, and everything that makes us *us* in our writing. That variation is good, of course, as far as it goes—writing would be hardly worth reading if it contained no personal variation.

But decades of cognitive science suggest that at a more profound and important level, some ways of writing work better than others. There are ways—call them general rules—to meet the needs of a variety of readers more reliably. As human beings, our brains are more alike than they are different, and the brains of readers benefit from a shared set of principles about writing. Some of these principles are quite small and familiar: begin each sentence with a capital letter. Others are more complex and more subtle and require more of you. Some are best wondered about in advance; some are better focused on in the revision process.

The following sections attempt to illustrate the kinds of things that great writers do. These rules aren't intended to stifle you any more than music theory points the way to better songs. Underneath all music is a universal set of rules that fit our brains. Writing is no different.

The following sections will share with you a set of ideas on how to be a better writer, both in building up our words and in editing them after we've written them. The advice rests on how our brains work to understand written ideas. The advice will hopefully make clear that there are practical rules for engaging in academic conversations with clarity and strength, and that these rules can be learned.

But first, we need to know what others have said.

SHARPEN YOUR SKILLS

1. Find a piece of writing you think is worth sharing with someone. Why is it worth sharing? What made it so memorable to you?

2. Who are your writing heroes? What makes them so? What inspires you as a reader? Perhaps write a brief paragraph exploring this idea for yourself.

CHAPTER 2

It Begins with Listening

What Have Others Said?

ONE OF THE SKILLS MOST CENTRAL TO WRITING IS
summarizing what others have said. Any writer on any topic, really,
is nesting their work within what others have done—even if that
writer doesn't acknowledge it explicitly. As we've already said, joining the academic conversation means we need to clearly identify
what has been said and how our ideas relate to that.[1]

Does summarizing the words of others weaken your own writing? Does using the ideas of other writers mean you don't really
know the topic well? Not at all. The mark of good academic writing
is an honest and clear admission that you are building your ideas

---

1   You may want to read Graff and Birkenstein, *They Say/I Say: Moves That
Matter in Academic Writing.*

on the shoulders of others. Not drawing on the ideas of others will almost always lead you to produce mediocre writing.

The Basics

The first step in joining the academic conversation, then, is to highlight what has been said already. To do this, we read important texts, make notes, highlight key sections, and prepare to write out simple, clear summaries of the main ideas inside. That sounds simple, and it is, but not all simple things are easy.

You want to ensure you capture enough of the author's original idea, and fairly, but also not so much that you are merely putting into your own words their entire argument. This balance can be hard to strike. As always, be guided by what the reader might need.

Let's consider an example. In this case, the Gettysburg Address:

Fourscore and seven years ago our fathers brought forth, on this continent, a new nation, conceived in liberty, and dedicated to the proposition that all men are created equal. Now we are engaged in a great civil war, testing whether that nation, or any nation so conceived, and so dedicated, can long endure. We are met on a great battle-field of that war. We have come to dedicate a portion of that field, as a final resting-place for those who here gave their lives, that that nation might live. It is altogether fitting and proper that we should do this. But, in a larger sense, we cannot dedicate, we cannot consecrate—we cannot hallow—this ground. The brave men, living and dead, who struggled here, have consecrated it far above our poor power to add or detract. The world will little note, nor long remember what we say here, but it can never forget what they did here. It is for us the living, rather, to be dedicated here to the unfinished work which they who fought here have thus far so nobly advanced. It is rather for us to be here dedicated to the great task remaining before us—that from these honored dead we take increased devotion to that cause for which they here gave the last full measure of devotion—that we here highly resolve that these dead shall not have died in vain—that this nation, under God, shall have a new birth of freedom, and that government of the people, by the people, for the people, shall not perish from the earth. (Lincoln)

Here's one simple summary that should suffice:

Abraham Lincoln, in the Gettysburg Address, reminded his audience that the Civil War was a contest for the soul of the American future. In commemorating the new war cemetery, he referred to the founding principles of the American nation, drawing on principles of justice and freedom, and of what he saw as his young nation's radical experiment in self-government.

Sometimes an even shorter summary will do. When putting many voices in conversation with each other, a string of short summaries might work. Here is an example of what that might look like:

Abraham Lincoln, in the Gettysburg Address, reminded his audience that the Civil War was a contest for the soul of the American future.

There is a lot going on in that sentence. It says something about the author, the main theme, and it even hints a little at the historical context. It is a better summary than "The Gettysburg Address is about the Civil War." Strive for full, economical summaries—lots of rich detail boiled down.

When summarizing, it makes sense to include something about the original author. Here is a worked example to consider:

"Skeptics Say, 'Do Your Own Research.' It's Not That Simple."
(Nathan Ballantyne and David Dunning)

A new slogan has emerged in the culture: "Do your own research." On internet forums and social media platforms, people arguing about hotly contested topics like vaccines, climate change and voter fraud sometimes bolster their point or challenge their interlocutors by slipping in the acronym "D.Y.O.R."

"Two days after getting the jab, a friend of mine's friend had a heart attack," a Reddit user wrote recently in a discussion about Covid-19 vaccines. "I'm not saying they're connected, but D.Y.O.R."

The slogan, which appeared in conspiracy theory circles in the 1990s, has grown in popularity over the past decade as conflicts over the reliability of expert judgment have become more pronounced. It promotes an individualistic, freethinking approach to understanding the world: don't be gullible—go and find out for yourself what the truth is.

That may seem to be sound advice. Isn't it always a good idea to gather more information before making up your mind about a complex topic?

In theory, perhaps. But in practice the idea that people should investigate topics on their own, instinctively skeptical of expert opinion, is often misguided. As psychological studies have repeatedly shown, when it comes to technical and complex issues like climate change and vaccine efficacy, novices who do their own research often end up becoming more misled than informed—the exact opposite of what D.Y.O.R. is supposed to accomplish.

Consider what can happen when people begin to learn about a topic. They may start out appropriately humble, but they can quickly become unreasonably confident after just a small amount of exposure to the subject. Researchers have called this phenomenon the beginner's bubble.

In a 2018 study, for example, one of us (Professor Dunning) and the psychologist Carmen Sanchez asked people to try their hand at diagnosing certain diseases. (All the diseases in question were fictitious, so no one had any experience diagnosing them.) The participants attempted to determine whether hypothetical patients were healthy or sick, using symptom information that was helpful but imperfect, and they got feedback after every case about whether they were right or wrong. Given the limited nature of the symptom information that was provided, the participants' judgments ought to have been made with some uncertainty.

How did these would-be doctors fare? At the start, they were appropriately cautious, offering diagnoses without much confidence in their judgments. But after only a handful of correct diagnoses, their confidence shot up drastically—far beyond what their actual rates of accuracy justified. Only later, as they proceeded to make more mistakes, did their confidence level off to a degree more in line with their proficiency.

The study suggested that people place far too much credence in the initial bits of information they encounter when learning something. "A little learning," as the poet Alexander Pope wrote, "is a dangerous thing."

Anecdotally, you can see the beginner's bubble at work outside the laboratory too. Consider do-it-yourself projects gone wrong. Power tools, ladders and lawn mowers are easily mishandled by untrained users who know just enough to put themselves in danger. A study found that U.S. consumer injuries from pneumatic nail guns increased about 200 percent between 1991 and 2005, apparently as a result of the increased availability of nail guns that were affordable for nonprofessionals.

Research also shows that people learning about topics are vulnerable to hubris. Consider a 2015 study by one of us (Professor Dunning) and the psychologists Stav Atir and Emily Rosenzweig. It found that when novices perceive themselves as having developed expertise about topics such as finance and geography, they will frequently claim that they know about nonexistent financial instruments (like "prerated stocks") and made-up places (like Cashmere, Ore.) when asked about such things.

Likewise, a 2018 study of attitudes about vaccine policy found that when people ascribe authority to themselves about vaccines, they tend to view their own ideas as better than ideas from rival sources and as equal to those of doctors and scientists who have focused on the issue. Their experience makes them less willing to listen to well-informed advisers than they would have been otherwise.

There should be no shame in identifying a consensus of independent experts and deferring to what they collectively report. As individuals, our skills at adequately vetting information are spotty. You can be expert at telling reliable cardiologists from quacks without knowing how to separate serious authorities from pretenders on economic policy.

For D.Y.O.R. enthusiasts, one lesson to take away from all of this might be: don't do your own research, because you are probably not competent to do it.

Is that our message? Not necessarily. For one thing, that is precisely the kind of advice that advocates of D.Y.O.R. are primed to reject. In a society where conflicts between so-called elites and their critics are so pronounced, appealing to the superiority of experts can trigger distrust.

The problem is compounded by the fact that outsider critics frequently have legitimate complaints about advice provided by insider authorities. One example might be the initial instruction from public officials at the outset of the Covid-19 pandemic that people need not wear masks.

Instead, our message, in part, is that it's not enough for experts to have credentials, knowledge and lots of facts. They must show that they are trustworthy and listen seriously to objections from alternative perspectives.

We strive to offer careful guidance when it comes to our own areas of expertise. Even so, some D.Y.O.R. enthusiasts may reject our cautions. If they do, we hope that they will nonetheless heed at least one piece of advice: if you are going to do your own research, the research you should do first is on how best to do your own research.

As in the earlier example, there are a few ways to proceed when summarizing. You might want a two-to-three sentence summary in order to capture most of the material you want to share with your own reader:

> **Nathan Ballantyne and David Dunning, writing in a recent column in the *New York Times*, argue that most of us tend to overestimate our own abilities, especially before we have reached the level of expert competence in a task. While they don't advocate merely trusting expert opinions, they do suggest we would do well to keep our own hubris in check; all of us are frequently wrong, especially when new at something, and we are often blinded by our own blindness. They suggest that "As individuals, our skills at adequately vetting information are spotty," so we should focus on "identifying a consensus of independent experts and deferring to what they collectively report."[1]**

And again, an even shorter summary might fulfill your needs:

> **Nathan Ballantyne and David Dunning, writing in a recent column in the *New York Times*, argue that it is easy to overestimate our own abilities, and so we would be smart to follow a reasonable consensus of experts; we need to beware overestimating ourselves at new tasks.**

---

1   You may want to summarize differently, of course. The specific summary of the original voice will depend to some extent on your use of it; you might choose to emphasize some elements over others. But always strive to be fair and capture the essence of what you take to be the author's intent.

Note the reference to the publication. Including the source strengthens it, as is shown with this example that omits it:

> **They say that we are all tempted to overestimate our abilities; trusting a thoughtful consensus of informed opinion is safer and will lead to better decisions.**

Why include the source? It gives the reader a more appropriate amount of information about the source. The reader requires this information to make sense of the information: Where does it come from? What are its merits? What is the publication? Including a reference to the author—at least on occasion—is very helpful for the reader. (As we will see later, writers suffer from the curse of knowledge—knowing things their audiences do not. It is best to spell out relevant details about those we choose to refer to where possible.)

More Advanced Ways to Summarize

One way to improve your writing, and how thoroughly you join the academic conversation, is to put a variety of writers on one topic into conversation with each other. To do this, highlight various writers and use summarizing verbs to introduce their major ideas. Here is a small example, drawn from a *New York Times* "Room for Debate" section on the most promising ways to improve schooling. This passage shows how brief summaries can be strung together to highlight the landscape of thought on a topic:

> **On the topic of school improvement, scholars are divided. Ripley, for example, *argues* that the key to better teachers is tougher teachers' colleges. She draws on the example of Finland to make the case that schooling systems that emphasize teacher training succeed in better measure. Mehta**

suggests we could consider training teachers like we do doctors, with extended residencies; doing so would increase the rigor of the training teachers receive, as well as improve guidance and supervision for those new to the profession. And Hanushek *claims* the most efficient way forward is to promote effective teachers and fire the rest. Without knowing with better clarity what actually makes a good teacher, he says we should be guided merely by the performance of the students in class, and use test scores to efficiently screen out ineffective teachers.[1]

Verb Choices

Which action word when summarizing makes most sense? It depends on your intention. Here are a few examples:

Argues

A classic verb when you want to clearly communicate to your reader the original author is making an argument (perhaps as opposed to a purely scientific claim): "O'Connor *argues* that classroom teachers ought to reflect the community in which they teach...."

Suggests

When the matter is slightly less clear, and you want to be a little more gentle, you might consider something like: "Smith *suggests* that the modern approach to drug policy is out of step with reality...."

---

1   See Ripley et al., "Room for Debate: How to Ensure and Improve Teacher Quality."

Emphasizes

This is a great word to use when you wish to highlight a debate or refer to many different voices on a topic. For example: "Sherman *emphasizes* that, when it comes to education policy, there are no clear answers."

Finds

Often used in a scientific context, or when any study has "findings." For example: "The authors of this study *find* that increased sleep improves grades...."

Agrees

Sometimes you want to highlight agreement between various voices on a topic. In that case, you could say: "Smith *agrees* with Naylor when he *argues* that _____."

Notes

A simple way to state a claim or view of an author is to say something like: "Hamilton *notes* that the field of history is filled with accounts of Napoleon...."

Here are a few other verbs that may be used to tell the reader how you intend to use the voices of others:

Challenges
Claims
Contends
Disagrees
Reminds
Warns

SHARPEN YOUR SKILLS

1. Open the newspaper and find an opinion piece (not a straightforward news article—something in the comment section). Summarize the author's main idea in one or two sentences.

2. Go to the *New York Times* "Room for Debate" section. See if you can summarize three different authors' views on a topic, using different summarizing verb choices for each.

CHAPTER 3

Quotation Integration

When Your Words Just Won't Do

SOMETIMES JOINING THE ACADEMIC CONVERSATION IS BEST done that others referencing the specific words of those you are reading. You might want to include a pithy or interesting phrase from another writer, or include a brief passage that indicates something of the personality of the sources you are working from. Summarizing is the principal way we use the work of others, but direct quotations, used judiciously, can be effective.

One rule should be followed: all quotations must be introduced in some way. The reader needs to know something about who the quotation belongs to. So, we should not do this:

Steven Pinker cares a lot about writing style. "I love style manuals" (1). His book is an homage to fine expression.

Did you catch the error? Without some introduction of the quotation, the sentence is jarring. Gerald Graff and Cathy Birkenstein call this "hit and run" quoting. As the writer, *you* know the circumstances in which Pinker's words appeared—you liked them enough to use them in your own writing—but it's not clear to the reader what is going on unless you do more to introduce the quotation. Here's one way of doing that:

> **Steven Pinker cares a lot about writing style. "I love style manuals," he writes in his book, *The Sense of Style*, itself an homage to fine expression (1).**

Notice that the quotation integration can happen, as it does in this sentence, at the end of a quotation. The reader can understand what happened, especially if the quotation is short, as it is in this case. These introductions can also act as natural places to introduce the person you are quoting.

> **Steven Pinker, a Harvard cognitive scientist, cares a lot about writing style. "I love style manuals," he wrote in his book, *The Sense of Style*, itself an homage to fine expression (1).**

In framing the quotation, you may also be able to add, as we do here, a little about the author and their credibility. As readers, we want to know why we should trust what we read; providing a small parenthetical phrase like the one above is a move in that direction.

One caution: avoid relying too heavily on direct quotations. In history or literature, long direct quotations are in some circumstances considered to be highly appropriate. In psychology, medical science, or economics, however, frequent direct quotations are considered to be out of place. In several disciplines, extensive quotation may be taken to suggest that you are unfamiliar with the material. In general, it is best to paraphrase the insights of others, using your own words and giving credit to the scholars you lean on. Only if the phrasing is unique, or if something important would be lost in paraphrasing, should you quote directly. Directly quoting facts should be strictly avoided.

CHAPTER 4

Basic Source Evaluation —Argument, Reasoning, Evidence

Moving Beyond Mere Summary

ANY WRITING THAT MAKES AN INTERESTING CLAIM ABOUT the world is a form of an argument. When we say "argument," we do not mean bickering or quarrelling or merely being difficult. We mean something like: *making a point and using evidence to support that point*. Scientists make arguments: when the Intergovernmental Panel on Climate Change describes how pressing climate change is, the scientists are making an argument and using evidence to support it. Any non-obvious point is really an argument (saying Brazil is a country might not be an argument, but then again, no one would write a book about that). Nearly all academic writing—and interesting writing generally—contains an argument.

One way to view nonfiction writing is to see within it at least three dimensions:

Argument:	**The main idea or proposition of a work. What is the main claim of the author? (New Jersey has an excellent schooling system.)**
Reasons:	**The notions that support the argument. What reasons convince us of the argument? (New Jersey's public school graduation rate is over 90%.)**
Evidence:	**The facts or data or information that lend support to the reasons. Why should we believe the reasons? (The National Assessment of Educational Progress—NAEP—rates New Jersey as significantly above average in both math and reading scores.)[1]**

Yes, this way of understanding writing can feel a tad artificial at times, but it is a useful way to approach texts, to understand the author's intentions, and to assess the success of their argument. It allows us to see individual parts of writing, almost surgically—and it helps us move beyond merely saying "I agree" to something more like "X's argument was well supported by evidence...."

Here's an example of what this looks like, based on a little article from the *New Yorker* by James Surowiecki called "The Cult of Overwork."

---

1   See, for example, "National Assessment of Educational Progress (NAEP)." New Jersey Department of Education, 2018, https://www.nj.gov/education/assessment/naep/.

Argument: James Surowiecki argues in "The Cult of Overwork" that the Wall Street obsession with pushing employees to work long hours, reflected in the broader economy, is likely not in firms' best interest. However, because of cultural factors like habit and tradition, the situation is unlikely to change.

(Notice that we can summarize the main idea in a sentence or two.)

> **Tip:** While it is unhelpful to adhere too rigidly to formulae, it is useful to consider nonfiction writing through the lens of Argument, Reasons, Evidence. Or seeing this pattern clearly makes the analysis of writing more efficient and precise—as well as less mysterious as you build your skills.

Reasons: Surowiecki's first claim is that young and ambitious knowledge workers in major investment firms have been overworked for a generation or so, routinely putting in fifteen-hour days.

He claims that overly demanding schedules have been a tradition of recent decades on Wall Street—it was expected of workers. New technology has tethered employees to their workplaces. And paradoxically, long working hours represent a kind of status, a sign for the employee that you are in an important industry and are yourself important. He also suggests that habit has played a role in this phenomenon: businesses have tended to keep doing what they have done in the past. In this case, overworked employees have become a tradition, according to Surowiecki, supported by both employee and employer.

He claims, however, that the cult of overwork is changing, that managers at major investment houses like Goldman Sachs have ordered employees to seek a better work-life balance. He argues that this would likely increase productivity since overworked employees are less productive than better-rested ones.

He ends on a doubtful note, though, arguing that the cultural pull towards overwork will be hard to reverse—even if it isn't productive. The psychological drive to overcommit to your job in these high-status industries is powerful.

(Notice that when we understand the chain or reasons, we trace them carefully and specifically. We describe the reasons briefly, but we don't assess them much or write much about the evidence. We are often plainly seeking to understand the main set of moves the author makes.)

Evidence: Surowiecki's main argument and line of reasoning are generally well supported, though there are some claims without sufficient evidence. His first claim, that workers in this field (investment banking, mostly) are overworked and have been for some time, is quite convincing. He cites a University of Pennsylvania study by a former Goldman employee detailing the long working hours and psychological fatigue. As well, a study from Harvard successfully establishes the phenomenon of overwork generally in the knowledge economy: "Ninety-four per cent worked fifty hours or more per week, and almost half worked in excess of sixty-five hours a week."

His second claim, that firms are changing, is supported by his reference to formal changes at Bank of America Merrill Lynch, Credit Suisse, and Goldman Sachs to reduce employee overwork. While there was no statistical evidence that the changes in policy saw a reduction in the number of hours worked, the changes in policy themselves act as meaningful evidence of his claim about the change in management practices.

His claim that firms would be wise to reduce working hours to increase employee productivity also has some support. For example, he cites the University of Pennsylvania study again to establish the destructive effects of overwork on employees. But he perhaps puts too great an emphasis on the view of one Goldman manager about the overwork–performance connection. Statistical evidence would be a more compelling way of establishing this central claim.

Other aspects of the article remain unsupported. For example, his speculations about the inner psychology of this employee overcommitment are bolstered by one sentence from Karen Ho's "Liquidated." But given the space constraints, the central claims have sufficient evidence.

(Notice that when we understand the evidence, we want to describe it briefly, and assess if it is compelling or sufficient to establish the reasons and main claim.)

SHARPEN YOUR SKILLS

1. Take the newspaper opinion piece you used a few pages back (p. 16). This time, write out in your own words the author's argument, their reasons, and the evidence supporting those reasons.

2. What kinds of evidence do comment writers in newspapers typically use? What are the advantages and disadvantages of those sources?

CHAPTER 5

Putting Ideas in Conversation—with Generosity

The Principle of Charity

THIS BOOK TRIES TO MAKE THE CASE THAT A VERY GOOD deal of interesting nonfiction writing is a kind of argument; you, as the writer, are saying, "This is the way it is, and here's why you should believe what I'm saying." I am hard-pressed to think of truly compelling writing that is absent entirely of the persuasive flavor. Scientists persuade, historians persuade, psychologists persuade, mathematicians persuade, social scientists persuade. Careful persuasion is the art of nonfiction writing, and the matter of that art is the grand set of ideas you encounter every day. In putting those ideas to use, the tone with which we engage in intellectual conversation is an important factor in our success or failure. The right tone will act as a key does in a locked door; the door will open with ease. But how can we characterize "the right tone"? How can you draw readers in and lead them to sympathize with your arguments? Above all, through charity.

We use the word *charity* to describe the most productive stance to take in any intellectual conversation. We could also use the word *generosity*—we should endeavor to be generous to those who might not hold our own view. Contrast the generosity of a principled scholar with the meanness of a schoolyard quarrel. As children, when we bicker, we are trying to get our own way, or to soothe our ego, or make ourselves feel important, or more commonly, experience the pleasure that comes with the self-assurance of "being right." We want to be king of the castle.

But good academic conversations aren't, thankfully, schoolyard shouting matches. They are careful and honest and filled with complexity and even a fair degree of doubt. Doubt is a delicate thing. Too much doubt and you wouldn't even bother to write anything at all. Gripped by a profound sense that you had nothing of value to say, there would be no point in writing anything. But the right kind of doubt—prudence might be another good word for it—makes all the difference in the world.

Remember: Adding to the existing academic conversation with grace and precision is more valuable than bellowing opinions only your friends might agree with.

There are a few good reasons to be charitable to the other side. First, being generous is a form of being humble and even cautious in the face of complex issues. Most questions that are worth answering have many subtle dimensions to them—they are not merely black and white. Should we pay reparations to groups that our society has harmed in the past? Should we allow citizens who have lived abroad for many years to vote in elections? Maybe, maybe not. Depending on the circumstances, there may be good reasons to and good reasons not to. No one has an infallible perspective, and reasonable people can disagree. Being charitable is an open acknowledgment that you might be wrong. And that is actually a position of strength, not weakness.

Another reason to embody generosity in your writing is that it allows you to more easily anticipate other ideas—even conflicting ideas—and respond to them in your own writing. We will develop this idea much more later in the book, but one of the advanced maneuvers in writing is to understand what those who might disagree with you would say. How might they see the world differently? What assumptions might they make that you did not? What evidence might they use? What might they see that you do not? Unless you think that your view is perfect, that your evidence is the only evidence that matters, that your ideas are perfect in their correspondence to reality, and that you have left out nothing, you have every reason to be charitable and generous to those who might disagree with you.

At least one other good reason exists for being charitable to those who might not agree with you: it is tiresome to read the prose of someone who is too convinced of their own view and overstates their case. The reader is exhausted when, sentence after sentence, you imply that only an ignorant person would disagree with you. You might have this feeling when talking to an older relative, maybe, at Thanksgiving dinner. Their expertise might be compelling, and they might even have a point, but at some point during their rant about "what's wrong with the world," we tune out. The conversation ceases to be an interesting exploration of an issue and ends up being a one-sided assertion. This is not the goal of our writing. We want to take a welcoming tone. Our readers are our friends, they are our equals, and we are speaking to them—not lecturing. We want to follow the advice of Adam Gopnik, one of the finest modern nonfiction writers: "The habit of 'sympathetic summary,' what philosophers now call the 'principle of charity,' is essential to all the sciences. It is the principle ... that a counterargument to your own should first be summarized in its strongest form, with holes caulked as they appear, and minor inconsistencies or infelicities of phrasing looked past. Then, and only then, should a critique begin" (104).

I lacked this charity as a young writer. It was one of my many sins. I felt the need to condescend to any reader who didn't have what I viewed as the common sense to see the world the way I saw it. It took some time to see the truth in the words of Socrates now 2500 years old that "the more I know, the more I realize I know nothing."

But don't be mistaken: the principle of charity does not mean we should avoid engaging with opposing views or that we should soft peddle our arguments. Not at all. It means simply that we are interested in pursuing the truth more than we are interested in winning points. It means that we accept that the world is a complex place, and that our ability to understand it will always be imperfect. We are human. We have biases. The least we can do is to be, to the best of our ability, honest about the limits of our own ideas. Granting others respect is both a sign of humanity and an indication that our desire to understand the complexities of the world is sincere.

Being charitable to "the other side" of an argument may also help us to realize that a great many arguments have more than two sides. It may lead us towards an exploration of possibilities we did not think of at the outset. Here's an example. Gabrielle was asked to write an essay on the topic, "Should the United States adopt a single-payer medical system such as Canada's?" Her immediate response was to say, "By all means! Even with Obamacare, many people in America lack medical insurance. To achieve fairness, we need a single-payer system!"

As she researched the topic, though, she did everything she could to be charitable to views on "the other side" of the issue.

As she did so, she realized just how many options there were. She couldn't research all the details of the possible systems; in the end she focused largely on the German and Italian systems as possible alternatives to either the Canadian or the current American model. And in the end, the position she ended up being charitable towards was the one she had originally held herself:

> Ultimately, this paper will conclude that the single-payer model may not be the one best suited to the United States—but along the way it will spend some time conceding that a single-payer model such as Canada's has many strengths. First and most obviously, a single-payer model would address the issues of glaring inequity that have plagued the American system. Second, a single-payer system would likely be considerably more efficient than the American system; Canadians have long enjoyed higher life expectancy and lower infant mortality than do Americans, even though their health system costs far less than that of the United States. While conceding the strengths of the single-payer system, though, this paper will also, crucially, ask whether a single-payer system is the *only* way to achieve better results than America achieves now.
>
> The health-care issue has long been sharply polarized, and many have been fixated on comparisons of the American system with the Canadian one. Many on the political left have held up the Canadian system as the alternative Americans should emulate, while many on the political right have denounced the Canadian system as "socialized medicine." Too few have looked beyond the Canadian single-payer experience to ask if other models might suit America better. Too often it has been assumed

that the only way to achieve universal health-care coverage is a single-payer system—"Medicare for all," as it is often called. But (as Pete Buttigieg, Joe Biden, and others have pointed out), a single-payer system is not the only way to achieve universality of coverage. It's quite possible to offer the American system of Medicare to everyone without insisting that everyone choose Medicare—without insisting, in other words, on a single-payer system for everyone. Such an approach accepts the fact that many Americans have a much deeper resistance than do most Canadians to anything that smacks of "socialism." Poll after poll shows that many Americans would prefer to keep their current coverage rather than be forced to switch to Medicare. Why force them, when doing so makes universal medical coverage in the US such a harder sell? As European experience has proven, one can construct a system in which basic medical care is paid for by the government and is available to everyone, but in which those who have the means to do so and the desire to do so may choose employer-sponsored and individual private health-care arrangements. And, on measures such as life expectancy and infant mortality, countries such as Germany and Italy have at least as good a record as Canada—and lower overall costs for health care.

You might hear the phrase "straw man"—that is, the tendency to make our opponents into mere caricatures or take the absolute weakest version of their argument or meaning. Avoid this at all costs. In omitting the best parts of others' ideas, intelligent readers will know you have only told part of the story. Readers will be more convinced of your view if it is nested within the best versions of others' ideas, the most generous parts of them highlighted, while still advancing your own ideas. Doing this requires care, but when done well, the strength of your persuasion will reach new levels.

SHARPEN YOUR SKILLS

1. Think of someone or something you disagree with. Perhaps it is economic (should we tax the rich more?), political (are conservative values better for society?), or something even more controversial. Write a brief paragraph taking the side of those who hold a position different, or even opposite, from yours. Find ways to use generous language. One test for getting the tone right: would a reasonable person who holds this belief agree with your characterization? Revise this brief paragraph until you get to that point.

CHAPTER 6

Topics and Research Questions

Adding Our Voice

FIRST THINGS FIRST: WE WANT TO FIGURE OUT WHAT WE'RE going to write about. When you have any writing assignment, be it for a high school history course or for a graduate dissertation, you need to have some direction. Sometimes, the topic is given by an instructor. If that's the case, some parts of the process are simplified, and you might be able to skip down a bit in this section.

But for most of us, we are given some general direction for our writing, sometimes only as much as a topic, and then it is up to us to develop it more. You might have a topic like "income inequality." But if you sat down to write about income inequality, you would likely either be gripped by paralysis, or, worse and more common still, just write aimlessly about whatever part of the topic feels important at the time. The reader would end up wondering what that paper is all about. In a paper that lacks definition, your research would be unsatisfying. Consider: What would you research under such a big topic? Would you just look at the first few results under a Google search of "income inequality"? Bad idea.

Student writing that lacks direction at the topic stage ends up being difficult to read—and often seems more like a rambling blog post or a late-night conversation. The answer: have a clear direction. If you do, all other stages of writing and revising will be more profitable. And having a clear direction begins with your research question.

What Is a Research Question?

Consider the research and writing process like a cycle. All inquiry begins with a curiosity, some question about how the world operates. The list of questions about life and our place in it are practically limitless:

- Does income inequality pose a challenge to democracy? (not sure yet);
- How necessary is homework for academic achievement? (probably useful, but the data isn't that clear);
- Is it a good financial investment for you to go to university? (likely, yes);
- Do video games increase violent behavior among players? (likely, no).

Research questions allow us to start looking for evidence from other writers, from subject experts, and from those who (in some cases) have dedicated their lives to the questions. Without the research question, we have no way to start looking; the question supplies a focus and direction. Consider the research question the first step in finding the academic conversation.

But one thing to remember: your first research question is likely not going to be very good. That is OK. More than that, it means you're on the right track. The research question process goes something like this:

1. We are curious about something;
2. We read general sources about it, typically using Google to find webpages (it takes some knowledge to make a good question);
3. Now that we know more, we refine our question;
4. We read better sources on those topics;
5. We might refine our question again as we learn more....

Research question development is cyclical. As we learn more, we ask better questions. With those better questions, we can learn more—and with greater and greater depth and precision. Hopefully, this process continues throughout your entire life; it is a story that shouldn't end.

What Makes a Good Research Question?

The best research questions have

1. Interest and relevance;
2. The right scale and size;
3. An available base of high-quality research to access;
4. Some room for debate—a good research question in the humanities and social sciences is typically not merely a factual question;
5. An openness: they do not assume the answer in the question.

Interest and Relevance

If you do a graduate degree, it is likely that you will have a meeting, sometime early on, with a graduate supervisor—a professor with whom you will work closely and who will help guide your research. If you're like most graduate students, you will have a few ideas about what you want to study. You might walk into the meeting confident that you'll impress the supervisor and that they will be excited about the direction you have chosen. And that might happen. But more likely is that you'll finish explaining your research questions, and then after a pause, the professor might say something like: "Why would anyone want to read that?" We need to be aware that what interests us might not interest anyone else. And for our work to be meaningful, it needs to find an audience.

One way to ensure that the question is worthy is by asking yourself if it has any real-world implications. If it affects people, especially lots of them, then it is likely interesting.

Scale and Size

Another common criticism of students' draft research questions is that the question is too big. Many initial research questions, especially those that emerge from students who aren't all that knowledgeable yet, are too big and broad to fit in anything less than three or four books.

Consider the question: "Do the rich always get richer?" In what country? Across what time periods? In which economic system? What data exists to answer it? A better question: To what extent have increased income tax rates prompted wealth flight? Or: What factors led to the failure of wealth taxes across Europe? Some good popular writing has been done on this latter question, sometimes quoting academics that you could find in the scholarly databases.[1] Using pop-

---

1   See, for example, Rosalsky.

ular sources to find important academics is a good move; it can help when navigating the scholarly databases by starting the search with a few authors.

Availability of Research

There are more great questions than we have answers to: that's the human condition. When developing a research question, be sure to check if the question is actually researchable. Many students are drawn to future-oriented questions. While very interesting, they are often not good research questions.

Consider this question, one that was asked during a research-question workshop in recent years: "In a future with gene editing, where parents can select for their children's height, strength, and IQ, how will childhood change?" What evidence exists on this topic? It hasn't happened yet. We can only speculate, and speculation isn't very valuable; everyone can speculate equally well and equally outlandishly. Without evidence, there is no way to judge the strength of the claim.

Or how about this question: "Will robots take all our jobs?" What possible evidence exists to answer this? A great question for humanity, but only time will tell. Again, we can't come up with anything more than speculation on future-oriented questions.

Room for Debate

Avoid questions that are so factual that the resulting paper would be little more than a recitation of facts. Are there still questions in this field worth thinking about?

An Openness

While it is tempting to assume the answer in your question, it is best to avoid doing so. On most topics, papers that begin with the sort of question that reads "Just how bad is X...?" tend to lack the necessary complexity, nuance, and fairness that the best academic writing demands.

Where Do You Find Research Questions?

No interesting research question comes from *merely* thinking about the topic. Many students believe that if they think hard enough, they will have some moment of clarity, some thunderclap will sound, and a great question will come to them.

This is not usually how it happens. Like most worthy things in life, the development of a good research question usually requires work. That also means, though, that every single one of you can develop worthy, interesting, and productive research questions. You need to read widely, have conversations with bright and curious people, and stay curious yourself. Question formation is part mystery, sure—our brains generate them automatically. But you'll develop more by seeding the ground through readings, podcasts, and conversation.

What Is the Debate on This Topic?

One of the best ways to understand the broader conversation on your topic is to quickly skim the earlier sections of a number of published papers on aspects of the topic. In nearly all academic work (but certainly in the social sciences), the writer's purpose in the early section of the paper is to allow the reader to understand what the current debate is on this topic. (You will do this in your work, too.)

A Research Question Checklist

✓ *Is my research question ...*

☐ interesting? Would someone want to read it? Does it engage in relevant, real-world, or otherwise important topics?

☐ the right scale? Could it be explored in the page limit? (Or would I need a whole book to answer it?)

☐ sufficiently complex, with the possibility of multiple dimensions, ways of understanding it, and viewpoints (an academic conversation on the topic)?

☐ capable of even being researched? Are there any high-quality popular sources? How about scholarly sources—have experts gathered interesting evidence on the question?

☐ on a topic that could, at least in theory, be debated (not purely a matter of reporting facts)?

☐ open and accepting of what I might find (not assuming an answer before I begin)?

SHARPEN YOUR SKILLS

1. Use the research question checklist to evaluate the following research questions. Which ones are any good? Which might usefully be narrowed down? Which ones are simply not suitable? Why?

   a. What chance is there of a Republican victory in the next American election?

   b. What is the best way to drive from Boston to Montreal?

   c. How much should high-income earners be taxed?

    d.   How does homework contribute to academic success?

    e.   Should governments stop subsidizing industrial-scale animal agriculture?

2. Develop a practice research question. Use the research question checklist to evaluate it. Be honest with yourself: the key to being a great writer and researcher is to be your own toughest and most honest critic.

CHAPTER 7

A Spectrum of Sources

Which Voices Should I Listen To?

WE SAID EARLIER THAT JOINING THE ACADEMIC CONVERSA-
tion begins with listening. The development of research questions
is no different. We should begin with other voices. Those voices can
come from writers and experts in various media. Let's consider the
various kinds of sources, what they offer, and their limits.

First, a word on the internet. We often get lazy in our thinking and imagine the internet to be a singular thing, a place in the
cloud or a very large computer, maybe, that holds information.
That conception is not accurate: the "internet" is not a noun that
describes one place, but rather the connectedness of various computers and servers. We don't really "search the internet" as much as
we use Google to locate files online. Type into Google a phrase like
"Chicago weather," and you'll get some responses: these responses
are, in the main, merely links to other servers (like those run by The

Weather Channel), and when we click on those links we are taken to files in some computer someplace. "The internet" is just a vast collection of these computers and files. The process is so seamless, though, that some students think Google itself contains all those files we look at; "Google" is a *directory*, not a source of information. We use Google to find pages that contain information, and we need to distinguish between good sources of information and not-so-good sources of information.

A Source Spectrum

First, let's consider the various kinds of sources you will encounter. There are, broadly speaking, two main kinds of sources: popular and scholarly, with a lot of gray areas in between.

Popular sources are likely the best place to start when we know only a little bit about something. When we say popular sources, we mean sources written for a popular audience. That phrase doesn't mean "popular" as in "lots of people like it"; it means "non-technical." It means that people might read it for pleasure. **Scholarly sources** are works of extended writing, often written, edited, and published by academic researchers for an audience of other researchers.

Source Type	Examples
General Websites/ Simple News	Random webpages
	Huffington Post
	Blogs
	Wikipedia
Quality Newspapers	*The New York Times*
	The Globe and Mail
	The Guardian

Source Type	Examples
General Interest Magazines/ Websites	*Time* *Newsweek* *Maclean's* *Vox*
Serious Magazines	*The New Yorker* *The Economist* *The Atlantic* *Harper's* *The New York Times Magazine*
Think Tanks/ Government Reports	Organizations like the OECD, the World Bank, or the UN often produce thoughtful, evidence-based reports
Scholarly Books Intended for a General Audience	*Enlightenment Now*, by Steven Pinker; *These Truths: A History of the United States*, by Jill Lepore
Scholarly Books Intended for Academic Readers	*Visual Cognition: Computational Models of Cognition and Perception*, by Steven Pinker; *"Myne Owne Ground": Race and Freedom on Virginia's Eastern Shore, 1640–1676*, by Stephen Innes and T.H. Breen
Peer-Reviewed Journals	*The Lancet* *The Canadian Journal of History* *Leadership and Policy in Schools*

Using the search term **"income inequality,"** let's see what kinds of sources we might find under each category.

General Websites

These sources are easiest to find, but the writing is typically unsophisticated and the evidence base often insubstantial. These sources aren't generally useful to you as a researcher.

> "Income inequality":
> *Investopedia*
> A pretty grim collection of factoids. Not really useful for much beyond (maybe!) learning a few key terms.

Quality Newspapers

Excellent newspapers are superb sources as a start. They can inform us of the national and international conversation on a topic and what some interesting thinkers are saying. These sources are often the first place to start looking, especially if your question relates to how the world is and what's happening in it.

> "Income inequality":
> *The New York Times*—"Study Shows Income Gap between Rich and Poor Keeps Growing, with Deadly Effects"
> This is a thoughtful article by Lola Fadulu that cites several economists, lots of relevant government data, and even some politicians who comment on the issue.

General Interest Magazines

Like newspapers, these general-interest magazines often provide factual reporting, mixed in with some opinion pieces. Longer-form journalism can be more in-depth and comprehensive than newspaper format allows.

> "Income inequality":
> *Time Magazine*—"The Top 1% of Americans Have Taken $50 Trillion from the Bottom 90%—and That's Made the U.S. Less Secure"
> This is a thought-provoking article that provides a good deal of context and background to a reader who might not otherwise be familiar with this complex topic.

Serious Magazines

Though not exactly "scholarly peer-reviewed" sources, these long-form magazines produce substantial, well-researched, fact-checked pieces that will typically trace the contours of the debate on important questions, and cite leading thinkers in the field (whose work you can then look up).

> "Income inequality":
> *The New Yorker*—"The Psychology of Inequality"
> Elizabeth Kolbert's discussion of inequality from a psychological perspective is well-written and comprehensive, drawing on the work of some of the biggest experts in the field.

Think Tanks or Government Reports

Some of the most interesting sources for our research are reports produced by governments, major institutions with research efforts (like the World Bank), or large academic think tanks. Take, for example, the OECD, a group of 36 leading nations. The OECD has many research interests; one in particular may bear mentioning.

Every few years they conduct their Programme for International Student Assessment, one of the most important research efforts in comparing the success of various schooling systems around the world. While not appearing in "peer-reviewed" journals, these reports are incredibly useful for anyone examining school systems around the world.[1]

The World Bank's Open Data site has a staggering amount of information on hundreds of topics ranging from climate change (CO_2 emissions by nation and globally), to health, to taxation, to gender, and so on. There are thousands of indicators, drawn from the most reliable sources available, free to use in your work. Consider it a statistical gold mine.

> "Income inequality":
> World Bank—*Income Inequality and Poverty*
> This source is written by an influential economist and draws both on important theoretical work as well as empirical data. It is as serious and complex as anything you might find in a scholarly monograph or a journal article.[2]

Scholarly Books

Often published by university presses, or authored by leading researchers for a wider audience, these books are a treasure trove of learning, and offer extraordinary reference lists with other sources to follow up on. Substantial books on your research topic can be as meaningful as a peer-reviewed journal—or even much more so.

---

1   See, for example, Schleicher.
2   This source is relatively old. Older sources can be very useful, but ensure they are still relevant.

And when you are an undergraduate, you will be expected to engage with the complex, long-form writing found in books.

"Income inequality":
Thomas Piketty—*Capital in the Twenty-First Century*
This book is regarded as a notable contribution to the field of economics. It is an exhaustive examination of the question of wealth and income inequality, drawing on vast troves of data.

Peer-Reviewed Journals

These journals are edited by experts in the field and publish articles and studies by other experts (typically, research professors who have devoted large portions of their careers to thinking deeply about these questions). They are often rich in data and evidence, and their reference lists (which can be 50 or more sources long), are superb places to find other research papers asking similar questions (as we'll see below).

"Income inequality":
The American Economic Review—"Economic Growth and Income Inequality"
This peer-reviewed paper was written by a Nobel-prize winning economist, Simon Kuznets, and has been cited over 17,000 times.

Who Should You Cite?

You should cite the best source for the purpose. Newspapers are excellent sources of "what people are saying" and helpful in setting the context for your paper. If you are writing about income inequality, and you want to point out that presidential candidates are discussing the issue, referring to the *New York Times* is an excellent idea. We often cite popular sources early on in our work to establish the relevance of the question, the "why would anyone read this?"

But in the body of the paper, where you examine the various scholars' views on the question, where you examine the evidence base for various claims, where you look at the question in the deepest way possible, a *New York Times* article of 800 words isn't going to cut it. In the belly of your paper, you want to cite experts—and the best experts you can find. Those experts are typically university professors or professional researchers, writing in peer-reviewed journals, scholarly books, and possibly government or think-tank reports. (We will explore the credibility of authors more fully in Chapter 9.)

What about Wikipedia?

Wikipedia is a wonder of the world, and nearly everyone—including scholars—consults it. It is a great place to go to learn about something that you have absolutely no knowledge of. Even though it is edited by volunteers and is free to the general public, Wikipedia is remarkably useful for humanity as a whole. But for serious work, it has major limits: it is rife with unattributed facts, plagiarism, and shoddy writing. Studies have frequently found that Wikipedia entries are lacking in quality, rigor, and accuracy.[1] Aside from consulting the reference list at the bottom of the page to lead you to further reading, I suggest avoiding Wikipedia for any academic purposes.

---

1   See, for example, Rector; and Kupferberg and Protus.

Return to Your Research Question—Often

Our goal in all academic work is to find and join the academic conversation. Like any conversation, we need to know what is currently being said, and who we should listen to. Your original research question was likely only a 7/10—at best. We require some direction in the form of a research question to begin at all (otherwise, we would have nothing to type into a scholarly database), but once we have learned a little bit more, we now need to ask if the original question makes any sense, or if it needs to be improved.

Remember: You're never really "done" with a research question; as you learn more, you ask better and better questions.

This process is iterative and cyclical. It continues throughout the writing process, and indeed over your lifetime throughout all your academic work. Each time you ask a question, and find a few answers, you get better at asking new questions.

SHARPEN YOUR SKILLS

Take the practice research question from Chapter 6. Find a source from each of the categories discussed above, and complete the chart on the following page.

	Citation	Ease of Reading for a Non-Expert?	Depth of Information and Evidence?
General Websites/ Simple News			
Quality Newspapers			
General Interest Magazines/ Websites			
Serious Magazines			
Think Tanks/ Government Reports			
Scholarly Books Intended for a General Audience			
Scholarly Books Intended for Academic Readers			
Peer-Reviewed Journals			

CHAPTER 8

Finding the Best Evidence

*Your Uncomplicated Relationship
with Google Is Over*

AS WE NOTED A FEW CHAPTERS BACK, YOUR RELATIONSHIP
with Google as a basic search engine needs examination. Google is
extraordinarily powerful, yes, but it is not suited to our task. It merely
foregrounds—based on a secret and powerful algorithm—what
public pages you might be interested in. But most of the highest-quality research isn't available in public pages: it is behind paywalls run
by the publishers that control academic journals.[1] This situation
is changing with the rise of open-access journals, but it's changing
slowly; we still need research databases to help us do our work.

---

1   This situation is a bit of a scandal. Scholars don't get paid for their writing in
academic journals, and the publishers of those journals make small fortunes. Why
do scholars keep publishing in these journals? Because establishing a record of
peer-reviewed journal articles is the key to getting and keeping an academic career.

Research Databases

A research database is a product that schools—including universities—pay for in order to gain access to the millions of academic papers that have been published. You search them, not unlike regular Google, and they give you results: in this case, academic papers, newspapers, graduate dissertations, and the like.

> **Remember:** In general, newer sources are preferable. Using a paper on climate change from the 1980s would be inappropriate (unless you were tracing the evolution of our thinking on the topic). Limiting your search by year can be very useful.

We will use three research databases: ProQuest, EBSCO, and Google Scholar. Each of these databases has their quirks and peculiarities, and on their own, each is incomplete. ProQuest and EBSCO are both somewhat clunky in their search methods. Google has trained us to be lazy, allowing us to type in a fairly confusing set of words and still receive meaningful results. ProQuest and EBSCO require much more careful attention to the search string. Use quotation marks on compound terms: if we don't use quotation marks around "climate change," for example, ProQuest will give us every time *either* of those two words appears in a source. You can use Boolean operators (and/or/not) between search terms. And both ProQuest and EBSCO allow you to limit searches to certain source types (peer-reviewed, for example), by year, by full text, and so on. The good news: if you find papers in these two databases, you will be able to read them.

Google Scholar, in contrast, has a much more friendly search system, more like the regular Google version. You can be kind of messy in your search, and Google Scholar will still return interesting papers.

But Google Scholar has a major weakness: because it is public and free, it will typically only show you that the papers exist, but not give you access to more than the abstract (remember—publishers want to get paid, and Google Scholar is free). If you are a student at a large research university, that's not a problem; these institutions' libraries provide access to the vast majority of scholarly articles. But the libraries of small institutions often cannot afford so many subscriptions and will thus be able to provide access to a much more limited range of material. If that's the case, you might try using Google Scholar to get a sense of the best papers on a topic, then use ProQuest and EBSCO to actually access full-text versions. This hybrid approach can yield excellent results.

Here's one other tip: it's worth registering with JSTOR, one of the largest of the digital libraries. Though most of the material it provides is behind a paywall, it allows any individual who registers with it to access a certain number of articles for free each month.

In any system you use, notice something helpful: once you find a scholar or two worth reading, you can click on their name, and you will be shown other papers by that author. In ProQuest and EBSCO, entries are also organized by subject, so once you find a few papers that intrigue you, search under that subject heading to find similar entries.

Mine the Reference Lists of Other Scholars

One of the simplest, efficient, and productive ways to become more of an expert on a topic is to mine the reference lists of other scholars. Every quality scholarly article is going to have some set of references at the end; you can—and should!—use these references for your own work. Exploring the references of scholars you admire isn't cheating or taking a shortcut: this is how scholarship works.

First, be sure you have an excellent paper. Ways to tell? Examining the credentials of the author, ensuring the paper is peer-reviewed, and tallying the number of citations it has are all simple ways to start to evaluate its usefulness. But then push further: What is the quality of the paper itself? Does it use a compelling method? Is it especially recent?

> **Tip:** Finding new opportunities for reading within the reference list of great pieces of writing is productive, efficient, and expected: it is one reason academics include such lists at the end of their work.

Next, look at the reference list. You will find 20–50 (or more!) sources. (On top of that, when the author of the paper you're reading references any work, they might even discuss the work itself, telling you what is interesting about it.) Find these papers in the scholarly databases, download them as PDFs, and you are well on your way. If you find even five decent scholarly papers on your topic, that will likely mean that the combined reference lists point to another 100 papers. While you will not have the time or the energy to take a look at all 100, you have no reason to think there "isn't any research on my topic...."

Some specialized papers will help in this regard: most empirical fields have "review" papers, where the goal is not to find new evidence but rather to systematically review what has already been said. For younger researchers, these papers are magnificently helpful.

Quality of Sources

When looking for sources, it is important to remind yourself that not all sources are created equal. Just as we would not believe just anybody and instead choose to rely on experts, so too should our research focus on using the best evidence.

We will explore this topic in Chapters 9 and 10, but for now, it is enough to know that we should tend towards papers appearing in established journals, written by experts in the field with a good publishing history, who use a rich set of mostly peer-reviewed sources. That is a good place to start.

SHARPEN YOUR SKILLS

1. Bookmark Google Scholar, ProQuest, EBSCO, and any others suggested by your instructors.
2. Perform simple searches for topics that interest you. Try "climate change" perhaps. Notice how you can limit the sources you get back by searching for scholarly and peer-reviewed articles. Get familiar with these tools.

CHAPTER 9

Establishing the Credibility of a Source

Not All Evidence Is Equal—
Show Why Yours Is Worth Citing

EFFECTIVE WRITERS ESTABLISH THE CREDIBILITY OF THE sources they use. Recall the goal: you are highlighting the most important voices on a topic with the goal of persuading the reader of your argument. Doing this—convincing a reader—is hard to do without giving them reason to believe. Yes, evidence is required. But in an era of seemingly abundant-but-questionable evidence, it's particularly important to provide your reader with some information regarding the credibility of your sources.

At this point in your writing career, there are two main ways to establish the credibility and validity of the research you cite:

1. By emphasizing the position of the person you cite
2. By emphasizing the quality of the evidence in the source itself

In popular sources, like leading newspapers, we frequently read about "a study conducted by so-and-so of such-and-such university finds that...." As far as it goes, this credential technique is fine. Mentioning that the research was produced by a professor is entirely appropriate in the *New York Times*, and pretty good, too, in your course work. As a younger researcher, this credentialing is an easy way to establish the merits of a source. Do it like this:

> **Beatty, a professor at Yale, finds that homework builds student confidence.**

Or

> **Stevenson, the head of technical research at the CDC, argues that viruses ...**

Notice in the examples above that a brief dependent clause to signal the merits of the source is all that's needed; an entire sentence (or worse, a string of them!) is unnecessary and distracting. And avoid providing this demonstration of credibility for every source you use. Doing so would be exhausting for the reader. Yet it is important—maybe once a paragraph, as a general rule—to establish the worth of key pieces of evidence for your reader. You might also read in popular sources, and write in your own work, that the research is "peer-reviewed"—this is also a perfectly fine way to establish that the citation meets a certain threshold of quality. You are telegraphing to your reader, without forcing them to look at the references, that your evidence base is serious.

But these sorts of credential discussions are also unambitious: in time, *all* the work you cite should be of the highest quality, and that will mean mostly peer-reviewed research written by professors at universities. When you do your PhD and are writing your literature review, you will not write "Pinker, a cognitive scientist at Harvard, found that ..." or "Loeb, a professor of history at the University of Toronto, argues that ..." The reason? *All of your sources will be scholarly*. And when all of our sources are scholarly, you need to focus on other criteria in order to establish the credibility of some studies over others.

Exploring the evidence, the second technique listed above, is the most interesting way to establish the merits of the citation. You can demonstrate the validity of the source to the reader by exploring the evidence. Here are a few hypothetical examples:

> **In a study of over 26,000 students, Smith found that homework was the single most despised part of schooling.**

Or

> **In an analysis of 1,352 original studies, Levinson finds that direct instruction is more effective than cooperative learning for introducing new concepts.**

Or, as an advanced maneuver, one could double-barrel the credibility by combining credential and research design.

> **In an analysis of 1,352 original studies, Levinson, the director of the Education Research Institute at the University of Madrid, finds that direct instruction is more effective than cooperative learning at introducing new concepts.**

Both of the scholars above are professors at universities, but by emphasizing the merits of the evidence in their papers, we are showing the reader something much more valuable: among the many voices I could cite on this topic, you are saying, I chose these because of the quality of the evidence they bring, the strength of their findings, and because of the magnitude of the impact they have made in the field. Put another way: professors disagree, so why should we listen to one more than the other? The evidence. Always be guided by the evidence.

Remember: The least stressful way forward in academic writing is to merely follow the direction of the best evidence.

A good rule of thumb: make four or five references to the credentials of the scholar, and four or five references to the quality of the study, per research paper. By doing so, you will ensure that your reader will have plenty of reasons to be persuaded by your research. That is the goal of discussing credibility: you are reassuring the reader that your evidence is worth listening to.

A General Rule of the Credibility of Evidence

In the broadest terms, we are looking for evidence with the following qualities:

- It is produced by someone with expertise.
- It is well sourced.
- The evidence base of the source is rich and relevant to the question at hand.

Sometimes, we describe these principles, especially in reference to the qualities of the author themselves, in a brief acronym.

Several different versions exist, including the very useful **RAVEN**:[1] Reputation, Ability to Observe, Vested Interest, Expertise, and Neutrality. In time, you will perform a brief mental mini-RAVEN every time you perform a search and consult a source. It will be part of your academic brainstem, coming automatically like breathing.

SHARPEN YOUR SKILLS

1.   On any topic of your choice, find two scholarly papers. What are the background, expertise, and merits of each author? How many papers of theirs can you find in the databases?

2.   In those same papers, what is the depth of the evidence base? Which of the two papers would you declare "more credible"? Why?

---

1   This helpful acronym appears in several places online, but notably within the College Board's guidance in the AP Seminar course.

CHAPTER 10

Evidence— Kinds of Studies

"Empirical"—Researching How the World Is

THE SORTS OF RESEARCH THAT ARE THE PRIMARY FOCUS OF this book are empirical in nature; that is, they focus on evidence from the outside world. For most of the questions you and I will ask in much of our studies, and life, we need to understand the conditions of the world around us.

We rely on evidence collected about the thing we're curious about. Want to know how fast the climate is changing? Collect scientific data from weather instruments and satellites. Want to know the lived experience of migrants fleeing a dictatorship? Ask them, either in surveys or in interviews.

So most of our work is "empirical." That is, we are asking how the world *is* and finding good sources of evidence to answer our questions. You won't be gathering the original research yourself at this point in your career—though you might be quite soon!—but your work will rely on empirical studies.

A very important note of caution: Do not expect that all academic work is "empirical."

There are many fields that are not very "empirical." As someone who studied philosophy as an undergraduate, for example, I can attest that many philosophical discussions—especially in some schools of thought—have little to do with how the world actually is outside our own experience of it. For example, if you are curious about human consciousness, there is a "hard problem" of actually understanding what it is like to be another person; this problem can't really be resolved in a study or a laboratory. Similarly, literary analysis isn't really an empirical field. When writing a paper on themes in a Shakespearean play, or on the treatment of race in *To Kill a Mockingbird*, your job isn't to discover how the world is, but to explore a text. Do not expect that our work here will mirror all work you will do in all academic courses. Some parts are the same, yes: a dedication to accuracy, to clear writing, to the defense of interesting ideas are constant across all fields. But the source of evidence will be different.

Lots of academics will quibble with the table on the following page, but it might be helpful to understand the kinds of papers you might come across when you enter academic databases. In databases like ProQuest, you will find papers of all of these sorts. You may draw on any of them, of course, and one sort isn't "better" than the next, but each sort has its best use. Let's explore the kinds of papers you will frequently see in your studies: original research studies, review papers, legal studies, and comment papers.

	Primary (Original)	Secondary (Synthesis)
Empirical	Research study	Systematic reviews Meta-analysis Book reviews
Non-Empirical (Theoretical)	Philosophical argument Legal papers Study of logic	Historiography (the study of what previous writers on the topic have said) Comment papers Literary analysis

Research Studies

Since most of our work is empirical, you will likely be relying heavily on peer-reviewed studies in your work. Depending on the discipline, the order of topics or paragraphs might vary in its particulars, but the general idea is the same. (For example, in historical papers, the convention is to avoid subheadings like the ones used in this book, and there isn't really a "research design" so much as a set of primary sources to be explored and understood; in my view, this is still largely empirical.) Here is the basic structure of most empirical academic studies:

Abstract

A brief summary of the study's main aims, findings, and next steps for future research.

Introduction

All scholarly papers have some sort of early section where they point out to the reader why this topic matters: what is interesting about it, why it needs further study, what this paper will add. The last section of the introduction is often highly instructive: it is frequently where scholars identify the most interesting questions (some that the study will attempt to answer).

Literature Review

Every scholar needs to nest their ideas within those of other scholars. It isn't just good form or proper manners; a literature review allows the reader some idea of how this particular paper fits into the broader discussion on the topic. A review of what has already been said provides the reader with the landscape of the topic. As well, the literature review will typically point to where gaps exist—the gap this study hopes to fill.

Research Design (Sometimes Called Methods)

This section typically describes the ways the researcher will gather new data. We will explore this idea more below; carefully understanding the research design is critical in evaluating the value of a paper's contributions to the field.

Findings/Results

This section reports what was found. Typically there is not a lot of analysis: the findings section tries to summarize for the reader the general set of data or evidence or information the study collected. In qualitative studies, this might be interview transcript excerpts. In quantitative studies, it might be tables of figures and data.

Discussion

This section attempts to clarify for the reader "what matters" about the findings section: what, if anything, can we conclude from this study? Often, this section will not just draw conclusions, but also revisit some other scholars' ideas to show how these findings fit with the work of other researchers. It may even suggest policy changes based on these findings.

Conclusion

Typically the most-read section after the abstract, this section is often a brief distillation of the most important findings, the limitations of the study, and hints at future directions. (Sometimes there are distinct sections explaining some of these elements—the paper's limitations, for example—but as frequently, these are rolled together in a Conclusion section.)

> **Tip:** A basic familiarity with the main types of research methods will allow you to quickly understand the possible contribution a paper might make to your own writing, as well as remind you of the limits of any piece of evidence. By its very nature, every research method excludes certain ways of viewing the world. Be aware of the insights and limits of evidence types.

WHAT KINDS OF RESEARCH DESIGNS ARE APPROPRIATE?

In research methods, there are two broad distinctions, and then many subcategories within those two large groups. Most research designs are either quantitative or qualitative. There are dozens of ways to subdivide quantitative and qualitative research designs, but the table below illustrates a few basic ones.

	Examples of Research Design/Method Subtypes
Quantitative	Observational
	Experimental
	Large data analysis (economic papers, for example)
Qualitative	Interviews
	Focus groups
	Text analysis
	Case studies

In general, quantitative studies rely on things that one could count and on the application of statistics. We see more of these studies in the hard sciences and in economics, as well as in the health sciences. Want to know if one drug is more effective at treating cancer?

Conduct a double-blind experiment,[1] gather data, and assess the question using statistics. Quantitative work often tests hypotheses. By its nature, such work can quickly gather data from across a large swath of people or circumstances—and is often intended to.

In some ways, we live in a quantitative age, but qualitative studies are very important and often overlooked. First, in many fields of inquiry, quantitative work can only come after qualitative work has been done. For example, if we were conducting a large survey on human wellness, we would have no idea what questions to include in our survey until we conducted some sort of qualitative work first (some academic papers in the social sciences are actually centered on the development of quantitative measurement tools from an earlier phase of interviews and focus groups). Second, while quantitative data can be gathered broadly across a wide variety of people and places, it is inherently thin—qualitative work can offer rich and thick description and a nuanced understanding of important phenomena.

Which is best? Neither; each offers its own distinct advantage and limitations. No one source or method could possibly reflect the entirety of the complexity of interesting phenomena. Use the most fitting source for the question at hand, try to triangulate using a range of methods, and always be explicit about the limits of your research.

---

1   A double-blind study is one in which neither the participants nor the researchers know who is in the treatment group, and who is in the placebo group. Such designs are typical in pharmaceutical research, and they lead to more reliable and valid research outcomes.

Review Papers

One of the unsung heroes of the academic publishing world is the "systematic review" paper. Some scholars will advance the work in a field by producing thoughtful syntheses of what other scholars have said before. These papers have the aim not of producing original findings, but rather of assessing the field and its recent work—a sort of "state of the field" on big questions. These review papers are gold mines: someone has made a map of the academic conversation for you, allowing you to get a sense of the landscape of meaningful debate and evidence in the field. Explore the reference lists of these papers.

Legal Studies

Many research topics (both qualitative and quantitative) may touch on legal questions; if that's the case with the topic you are working on, you may find yourself reading legal studies. Such papers deserve special mention; they are a little different than papers in a lot of fields. First, because law is a practical profession, these articles are typically not blind reviewed by peers. Second, the authors typically don't hold PhDs. Third, the papers contain more argument and comment than evidence. Don't let these peculiarities deter you: if you are curious about legal questions, these papers are very suitable.

Comment Papers

Sometimes journals will include editorials at the beginning of their volumes. Typically written by the board of the journal, these papers address big questions in the field, but typically with reference to values, not empirical evidence. You will find these kinds of papers in the body of the volumes, too, often from leading lights of a field on major topics. Sometimes papers will be in a "comment and reply" format, where an argument between scholars is explicit—they quarrel within the pages of a journal. These papers can be useful if you want to understand discussion and debate in a field and learn about the views of some of the important scholars.

How to Skim Well

Especially when you're starting out, no one expects you to sit down and read dozens of academic papers, word by word, as you conduct your research. You are expected to skim! You *will* read the key pieces of evidence in your paper very carefully, especially as you get further into the topic. But at first, you really must skim to get a sense of a broad range of academic papers and studies on the topic. The need for quickly skimming a paper is precisely why research studies are crafted in such formulaic ways.

Starting with the abstract is always a good idea, but after reading the abstract, I like to skim the introduction and look at transitions between sections to get a sense of things. I invest more in reading the methods (or research design) section—it is often neglected by readers but is very instructive in understanding whether I want to cite the paper—and the findings section, which is the most central repository of actual evidence.

SHARPEN YOUR SKILLS

1. Find one empirical study on any topic that seems interesting. Complete the table on the following page using the study.

Section of Paper	Brief Description of the Main Points
Introduction	
Literature Review	
Research Design (sometimes called Methods)	
Results or Findings	
Discussion or Analysis	
Conclusion and Future Directions (if it exists)	

2. See if you can find a paper of each of the types mentioned in this chapter on a topic you are interested in. Make a list of these papers—they might come in handy later in our extended writing.

CHAPTER 11

Gathering and Organizing Evidence

Invest Now, Reap the Benefits Later

ONCE YOU START EXPLORING THE RESEARCH DATABASES, you soon will be flooded with documents and ideas, and before long, it's likely to feel a little overwhelming. The path out of that drowning feeling is to adopt a system of organization.

How to Organize Your Sources

In the old days, students would lay out all the books they wanted to use in their paper, covering their kitchen tables. They would nip in and out of each book, gathering what they needed, and writing or typing as they went. Using this system, one felt like part hunter, part mad genius, fingers whirling, being "efficient." Or so we thought. The reality: our papers were poorly thought out, the evidence weak, and the final result quite lacking.

The modern version of this practice is the multiple-tabs-open-in-our-browser approach. Locate a series of papers online, keep them each in their own tab, and leave those tabs open for weeks while readying ourselves to write. Many problems occur: we lose the tabs, we think we had sources we don't, and we end up scurrying at the last minute to fill in the gaps.

The Solution to the Problem of Stressful Disorganization Is Easy

1.   When you find a source, any source you *might ever* use, save it as a PDF and put it in a folder with all sources for this project. PDFs are easily saved and searched.
2.   When you save the source to a local folder (or better yet, a Google Drive folder), ensure you rename each file in a useful and consistent way. (I suggest abbreviated title and scholar. So, the article, "Blending Classroom Instruction with Online Homework: A Study of Student Perceptions of Computer-Assisted L2 Learning," by Sagarra and Zapata, becomes BlendingClassroomInstruction_Sagarra.)
3.   Export the proper bibliographic citation *when you save the file* into someplace easily located later. I suggest a Google Doc.
4.   Use a note-taking template when you assess and explore a source. See the next page for an example.

One Helpful Note-Taking Template

You will find what works for you, yes, but consider something like this when gathering notes from your sources:

Kohan, Andrea, and Brian P. O'Connor. "Police Officer Job Satisfaction in Relation to Mood, Well-Being, and Alcohol Consumption." *The Journal of Psychology*, vol. 136, no. 3, 2002, pp. 307–18. *ProQuest*, http://search.proquest.com/docview/213835897?accountid=36317.

Topics or Keywords: alcohol, job satisfaction, mood, police, well-being	Sources of Evidence:	What Makes This Paper Worth Citing? (Credibility)
Key Ideas and Conclusions: (Include page numbers!)		

The template above is useful for taking notes on any given source. The one below is useful to get a bird's eye view of all your sources and how they might fit into your paper:

Source (in an Accepted Academic Format)	Why Is This Source Valid or Credible? (Why Would I Cite It?)	I Use This Source to Establish ...?

The key here: be disciplined as you gather research. It will pay dividends later, and save you a lot of time and frustration. Not doing so—just keeping tabs open on your browser—will certainly lead to a more challenging and painful time in writing, and a weaker paper in the end.

SHARPEN YOUR SKILLS

1. Make a Google Doc of some helpful templates. Keep this list handy. Star it in your Drive. Prepare a folder in your Google Drive for papers you might save. Commit to putting them all in one place—and naming them consistently!

CHAPTER 12

The Development
of
Your Argument

You Have Researched:
Now What Do You Have to Say?

THINK OF ALL YOU'VE DONE THUS FAR. YOU HAD, SOME time ago, a curiosity. We called that a research question. You did more reading, perhaps consulted the research databases, and found that your original question was good, but having learned more, you could improve it to better reflect the kinds of questions being asked by leading voices in that field. Then, you continued to plumb the depths of ProQuest, EBSCO, and Google Scholar, collecting lots of papers; the ambitious among you might have taken a quick look at more than 30, perhaps, and settled on 15 or more to use in your paper. You downloaded PDFs of those papers and neatly organized them. You took notes about these papers and studies, understanding what made them credible and worth citing—and even how you might use these papers to support your growing ideas on this research question.

That's a lot of work, yes, but now comes the fun part: you get to tell the world what you have learned.

What Is the Story You Want to Tell?

In academic circles, we often use the word argument to mean a set of ideas supported by evidence. The core of your argument is your main point, what we sometimes call a thesis statement.

Thesis Statement Guidance

- The best thesis statements are clear, direct, and compelling. They say something important *about* the topic, not merely announce the topic.
- They stake a position: you say something about the world.
- That position could be disagreed with, at least in theory. Purely factual thesis statements aren't very productive.
- They are the right scale—you could address this question in the space allotted.
- They *can* be more than one sentence.
- They do not *need* to connect to every paragraph in the body of your essay, but some sense of cohesion with the body of the essay is important.

Some Less-Than-Great Thesis Forms

1. **Less-than-great**: "This paper will explore ..."

   Here's the problem: The reader only knows the topic of your paper, nothing more. Using this sort of thesis statement is a bit like saying, "At this restaurant, we serve food."

Improved version: "This paper will explore the question of _____, ultimately concluding that _____."

2. **Less-than-great:** "The government should pay police officers more ..."

    Here's the problem: This question relies on a value, not really a set of facts or evidence.
    Improved version: "Evidence suggests that police departments with high wages are more effective at reducing crime ..." Find some way to make the topic rooted in the evidence, rather than merely a value judgment.

3. **Less-than-great:** "There is no doubt that money buys happiness ..."

    Here's the problem: This question is so big you would require a few books to establish it fully.
    Improved version: "Evidence suggests that higher incomes drive up self-reported happiness levels, but only to a point. Happiness is also shaped in important ways by social connections and self-perceptions ..."

You might not finalize your thesis statement until you are fully finished with the body of your paper; sometimes it takes the act of writing to clarify the fine details. But all writers need some target to aim for before writing. Your argument is the target.

SHARPEN YOUR SKILLS

1. Assess each thesis statement below.

Statement	How Could It Be Improved?
This paper will examine the problem of human trafficking.	
What is the issue with genetically modified organisms?	
China has become the world's great economic superpower.	
Video games should be banned for those under 18.	

CHAPTER 13

The Structure
of the Paper

*A Recipe for Clear
and Effective Paper Writing*

ALL GOOD WRITERS PLAN THEIR WORK. WE HAVE AN IMAGE in our brains of the writer sitting in front of a computer screen, typing away, starting at the beginning of a piece and writing all the way to the end. But this is not how humans write—at least, not most of us. You might be possessed of a mind that can plan as you go, working out all your ideas as you type, without delay, confusion, or collapse. You might think you function best by merely opening a series of tabs on your Chrome browser, each with a source you want to cite, and jumping back and forth between them all, part composer and part conductor, magically weaving all these notes together to form something amazing at the end. But this rosy picture bears no resemblance to reality.

Before we write something of consequence, we need an outline. An outline is merely a provisional plan, subject to change as we learn more as we write. But if you invest time and thought in creating an outline, it will change your writing profoundly. Even if you are good at generating ideas, you will certainly find it instructive to shape those ideas into a plan and put that plan down on paper. Articulating a plan will force you to work out ideas, ensure that the ideas banging about in your head are as good as you think they are, and capture them so you don't forget.

This is not to say that when we plan, we forgo all sparks of creativity and imagination: on the contrary, a plan can allow us to be more creative, more "in the moment," and ensure that our work is lively.

A word on brains and multitasking: we can't do it as well as we think we can. In what is now a famous study, researchers from Stanford University found that heavy multitaskers were less capable of focus, and more distracted by outside stimuli (Ophir et al.). Imagine if someone asked you to juggle while solving complex math problems—it is much easier to do one thing at a time. By putting down the flaming knives you were juggling, your brain can focus on the math. By making an outline, your brain can focus on planning and organizing without having to do the actual writing at the same time. Give your brain the focus it needs to do its best work: make an outline that allows you to reach your fullest expression.

Remember the Curse of Knowledge

Earlier, we introduced the idea that we, as writers, are beset by the curse of knowledge—that is, we assume all people know what we already know, and we fail to write with the audience's needs in mind. We assume our audience knows things they probably don't; this curse of knowledge leads to confusing writing, or at the very least, writing that fails to achieve what we want it to do: persuade the reader, and, in some meaningful way, allow the reader to have the view of the world that you have.

Adam Gopnik, in his fine book *Angels and Ages*, points out that few virtues are as important as being critical of your own writing. We need to be critical of our own work, see its imperfections, needle it, prod it, and show all of its cracks and crevices. We need to do so not to be unkind to ourselves, but because doing so is honest: all of our ideas are imperfect, have limits, and sag in spots. Being able to identify those weaknesses serves to strengthen your writing, not undermine it.

A Good General-Purpose Structure
for Academic Writing

With all of this in mind, what is a good general approach to ensure we give the reader what they need?

Section	Basic Mission
Introduction	• Provide context for the topic • Stress the significance and relevance • Provide your argument (thesis statement) **"What is the topic, why does it matter, what is your main point?"**
First Few Body Paragraphs	• Background detail (if an average reader might need it) • Perhaps a further exploration of the significance and relevance **"How can you bridge from intro to body of argument?"**

Middle Body Section	• Explore the important subtopics to give the reader your understanding • Support the argument with evidence • Put scholars in conversation • Assess and explain the meaning of the evidence **"What evidence is needed to explore the topic and persuade the reader?"**
Counter Thesis Body Paragraphs	• Consider alternative views and evidence that runs (or might seem to run) counter to your argument • Highlight the limits of your evidence **"What might an intellectual opponent say? How can I build room for objections in my paper?"**
Concluding Section	• Summarize to remind the reader of the most central points • Extend your argument to consider the consequences or implications of your ideas **"What should your reader remember from your paper? And what are the consequences of your argument: how will the world be different if we accept your conclusion?"**

There are many possible ways to structure a piece of academic writing, but to achieve our mission—the development of a clear argument based on a good research question that also addresses limits and implications—the above format is a great starting point. All models are inherently limiting; move beyond this one when you feel you have outgrown it.

How Much Detail Should I Have in My Outline?

When considering the level of detail required in a truly helpful outline, I suggest the following analogy: your outline should be a recipe others can follow. A lot of outlines are too skimpy to really serve you well as you move forward. All of us assume that we can hold more details in our head than we actually can. We also tend to assume that those details are sensible, clear, and coherent (they often aren't). Make your outline as detailed as a recipe—not just an ingredients list, but a plan that describes in detail the *how* as much as the *what*.

Here is one model you might find productive:

Research
Question

Thesis

1st Paragraph	**Key Theme or Topic Sentence:** **Evidence:** (Refer to specific studies) **Explanation:** (How do the evidence and subtopic matter?)
2nd Paragraph	**Key Theme or Topic Sentence:** **Evidence:** (Refer to specific studies) **Explanation:** (How do the evidence and subtopic matter?)

3rd Paragraph	**Key Theme or Topic Sentence:** **Evidence:** (Refer to specific studies) **Explanation:** (How do the evidence and subtopic matter?)
4th Paragraph	**Key Theme or Topic Sentence:** **Evidence:** (Refer to specific studies) **Explanation:** (How do the evidence and subtopic matter?)
5th Paragraph	**Key Theme or Topic Sentence:** **Evidence:** (Refer to specific studies) **Explanation:** (How do the evidence and subtopic matter?)

Conclusion

This sort of model is sometimes referred to as a plan rather than an outline. Some writers find it helpful to create *both* a very rough initial outline *and* (at a later point) a paragraph-by-paragraph plan, while others prefer to tweak and tighten their initial rough outline as they proceed.

CHAPTER 14

Using Evidence Well

*What Does It All Mean,
and How Does It Fit Together?*

YOU HAVE GATHERED A LOT OF EVIDENCE IN YOUR STUDIES.
Now it's time to use it. Your reader is going to need to be persuaded, and to that end, you will need to showcase and highlight important books, studies, comment papers, and reviews of previous research. How do you ensure that your evidence presents a coherent, cohesive argument?

A Basic Formula for Using Evidence

Remember two things when using evidence. First, your job here is to lead your reader to the same understanding of the issue you have, after all of your research. And second, brains require help to understand relevance. When you use evidence, keep these two considerations in mind.

What we tend to do in our first drafts of writing is to have a decent topic sentence, fill the body of each paragraph with facts, references, and citations, and assume the reader understands everything. The reader will need more help—the curse of our own knowledge stalks us everywhere.

Many ways exist to ensure the reader gets what they need from your evidence, but this general-purpose formula works in many circumstances:

Introduce scholar + discussion of source credibility + explanation of evidence + commentary.

Here is a worked example:

"Scholar, a professor of _____ at _____, finds in a 12-year study of 14,314 adolescents that candy increases happiness by 16 per cent. This evidence illustrates the relationship between diet and joy and suggests that _____."

Introduce Scholar	"Scholar,
Discussion of Source Credibility	a professor of _____ at _____, finds in a 12-year study of 14,312 adolescents that candy increases happiness by 16 per cent.
Explanation of Evidence	This evidence illustrates the relationship between diet and joy ...
Commentary	and suggests that _____." (Some exploration of an idea related to your argument.)

One need not work this hard to use evidence. Many (most?) of your references will be presented in passing, establishing facts and quickly highlighting other voices in the field. They will look more like this: "Pinker demonstrates that, contrary to popular opinion, violence has declined across the world in the past few hundred years (*The Better Angels*)." But perhaps once a paragraph, or at least three or four times in a paper, really explore the source and its evidence.

Underscore the Meaning of Evidence—and Connect It Back to Your Argument

One way to help the reader come to your understanding of the issue is to be sure to underscore the meaning of the evidence. In the example above, note the commentary sentence at the end. You need some way to show the reader not just what evidence exists, but *why this evidence matters and how it supports your overall argument.*

Some sentence templates that will stress to the reader how your evidence matters:

These findings highlight the importance of ...
These findings suggest that ...
This evidence points to the importance of ...

Most significant pieces of evidence should be unpacked. What's the right ratio of passing references and deeper references? Hard to say. Some sections of some papers exist to provide the reader with factual background or context. In those cases, more glancing use of sources would be appropriate. In other cases, though, especially in the central part of the paper where you are establishing your argument, ensure your evidence is explored fully.

A good rule of thumb is that at least once or twice in the paragraphs where you establish your argument, be sure to fully unpack the evidence: stress the credibility, explain the evidence fully, and connect with commentary back to your own set of ideas.

Linking Sources Together—
Stress the Academic Conversation

One of the important techniques of scholarly writing, when highlighting the academic discussion on a topic, is to put sources in explicit conversation with each other. Here is an interesting example that discusses the usefulness of gamification in schooling:

> The use of gamification in learning has shown mixed results. For example, Hanus and Fox (2015) found that students in a gamified course felt less motivated, satisfied, and empowered than those in a non-gamified course during a 16-week semester. On the other hand, Domínguez and colleagues (2013) found that students who completed the gamified course performed better in practical assignments and in overall score than those in a non-gamified course. This may be due to the fact that these two studies were gamifying different types of courses: one is social science and the other is computer science, and extrinsic awards such as badges may have undermined students' intrinsic motivation in the social science class, as students were already intrinsically enjoying the course. Nevertheless, the inconsistent findings suggest that gamification has the potential to improve learning, yet its effectiveness may be influenced by factors such as the specific implementation. (Jiang 2)[1]

---

1 This is actually an excellent synthesis paper that does a wonderful job of integrating many scholars' voices.

The topic sentence communicated clearly the intention of the paragraph. The sentences that follow highlight a few scholars' views. And note the explicit language in the transition phrases: "For example, Hanus and Fox (2015) found.... On the other hand, Domínguez and colleagues (2013) found...." The goal here is to communicate to your reader that there exists a broader conversation on this topic—and to give your reader a sense of how the various voices fit together. Some phrases indicate agreement ("similarly"), some indicate disagreement ("conversely"), some hint at a complexity of opinions "echoing the findings of Scholar, Scholar adds to the picture by...."

The goal to aim for: your reader should understand that there are a series of important voices on your question and that they fit together in important and coherent ways. Your job is to tell that story and ensure your own voice adds rich commentary.

A Basic but Important Question—When Should I Cite?

Many students wonder when they should cite research. These students know that citing is important, but they aren't sure when it should be done. They do not want to commit academic dishonesty, and they fear they will "accidentally plagiarize."

Good news: the rule is simple. You need to cite in two instances.

1. You must cite when you quote directly. As stated elsewhere, be judicious with the amount of direct quotation. Unless the phrasing is unique or you want to draw attention to an important turn of phrase, it is far better to paraphrase. Never cite a plain fact that is widely known and generally accepted.

2. You must cite when you put forward a striking idea that is not your own or introduce a piece of information that is not a commonly known fact. Ask yourself: would a reader want to see where that idea or fact came from? If you are writing that "D-Day occurred on June 6, 1944," then a citation isn't necessary; this fact is widely known, and no reader will want to know where you got it. But if you wrote "The Canadian forces suffered 340 deaths and 574 casualties taking Juno Beach as part of Operation Overlord ('Canada')" the reader may well want to know where that data came from. Similarly, if you are paraphrasing an idea unique to a particular scholar, you need to give credit. If you write, "Hitler did not set out to conquer Europe; he was an opportunist who responded to situations as they arose," you may not strictly speaking be plagiarizing, but nor are you putting forward an original idea. Much better to write this instead: "It was A.J.P. Taylor who first argued that Hitler did not set out to conquer Europe, but was rather an opportunist who responded to situations as they arose." As made clear elsewhere, this giving of credit exercise isn't arbitrary, nor does it weaken your writing. You actually strengthen it by showing you are nesting your own ideas within the bright lights that have gone before.

There might be paragraphs—especially in the evidence-heavy middle sections—where you cite frequently, in some cases every sentence. This is not a problem. As you become more aware of what is and is not commonly known, you might get more sophisticated about when to cite. For now, err on the side of more frequent citation.

SHARPEN YOUR SKILLS

1. Find a paragraph in a paper you have been reading that puts scholars in conversation well. It could be from a published paper, a newspaper or magazine article, or even a friend's school paper. Highlight or underline the voices.

2. What are the best kinds of transition phrases to join these voices? Take a look at a few papers and make a list of your five favorite transition phrases, including ones that might signal agreement, disagreement, complexity, or qualified support.

CHAPTER 15

Making Our First Draft Better—Follow the Basic Rules of English

"Easy Reading Is Damned Hard Writing"[1]

WRITING IS NOT EASY, AND IT CAN BE OVERWHELMING TO worry about all the rigid rules of composition in the midst of writing itself. You can give yourself permission, if it is helpful, to write the first drafts in an easy and somewhat casual manner, following your intuition and instincts, watching as the sentences unfold. Being less self-critical in early drafts will likely help your best ideas flow before you cut them down in haste. But eventually, you need to revise your work.

My own journey to this conclusion came relatively late: the first term of university, probably. The problem had started much

---

1   This phrase is often attributed to Nathaniel Hawthorne, but it may not have originated with him. See the fascinating discussion at Quote Investigator, "Easy Reading Is Damned Hard Writing."

earlier, of course. I owe a lot to my elementary and secondary school teachers. They were hardworking and supportive. But when I was in school in the 1990s, we were still living with a well-intended legacy of what we might call the de-stultifying of writing instruction. While the story isn't quite true, it goes something like this: before the reforms of the 1960s, composition was taught by uptight grammar freaks who cared more about pedantic rules than about free expression. Liberated from that way of thinking, young people could use language more freely and drop sentence diagrams and discussions about mechanics.

I earned good grades, and I was praised for being a good writer, but there were limits to the skills I could pick up by merely *watching* how language was used. I lacked any formal sense of how writing actually worked: I didn't know much about the parts of speech or how they best fit together. I think I might have believed, at least subconsciously, that there were really no agreed-upon rules of writing. I had, to some extent, lived the results of the previous generation's reforms.

And it did not always go well. I often tell the story of the first papers I got back in university. My new instructors had heavily criticized my writing style. I was not very used to this feeling of someone pointing out faults in my writing. Worse still, they used terms I had not even heard in high school. What, I wondered, was the passive voice, and why was it such a problem? I recall feeling my neck get hot. I realized I would have to open those writing style books my instructors had placed on the reading list. Thank goodness I did. The first book I turned to was *The Elements of Style*, by William Strunk and E.B. White. (It is still the most important book on the topic, and I include a large section on it in Appendix A.)

Here are a few more things to keep in mind when it comes to the process of revision: first, writing is mostly rewriting; second, you need to meet the reader where they are, and that requires understanding what they know and don't know; third, a few basic rules of grammar go a long way in meeting the needs of the reader. Steven Pinker, the Harvard cognitive scientist and polymath, has written widely on what it takes to be a clear writer. Not surprisingly, he emphasizes revision. He puts it like this:

> I am told there are writers who can tap out a coherent essay in a single pass, at most checking for typos and touching up the punctuation before sending it off for publication. You are probably not one of them. Most writers polish draft after draft. I rework every sentence a few times before going on to the next, and revise the whole chapter two or three times before I show it to anyone. Then, with feedback in hand, I revise each chapter twice more before circling back and giving the entire book at least two complete passes of polishing. Only then does it go to the copy editor, who starts another couple of rounds of tweaking. (*Sense of Style* 76)

If Pinker, one of the finest scholarly writers of our generation, requires this much revision, mere mortals like you and me will need at least as much.

Why is it so hard to write clearly? Again, Pinker is helpful. He points to the curse of knowledge: "The main cause of incomprehensible prose is the difficulty of imagining what it's like for someone else not to know something that you know" (57). When we write, we need to remember that *the reader has only the words you give them, so we need to give them what they need*. When we write, and even when we read what we've just written, our brains do something more than just reading: we project onto the paper lots of things that aren't there. This not-there-but-in-the-background material includes knowledge, facts, ideas, and even words that aren't there. (Anyone who doubts this should conduct an experiment: if you can, open an email from five years ago. If you're anything like me, once you've lost the context of the moment, you won't recognize your own writing, and you will wonder what on earth you meant.)

Our job, then, is to ensure in the revision process that we consciously and carefully attend to the needs of the reader. Frequently, these needs are met by simply using the basic conventions of our language.

The Basics

You can read very lovely, very long, and very complex style guides that discuss all the uses of all the tools in the grammarian's toolbox. This book does not approach all the rules that would cover all of the writing you might ever take on. But in this time and place, I think it is useful to provide a little vocabulary to understand the basics: as with most things, understanding the fundamentals is the wisest and most economical way to start.

Rules of Clear Composition—The Short List

1. All sentences should begin with a capital letter. Only capitalize proper nouns after that.
2. Subject + verb + object = clear, simple, direct writing. This is a good pattern to adopt.
3. Punctuation guides the reader through your ideas. Master the basic punctuation marks.
4. Periods separate sentences and ideas from each other. The reader needs breaks to digest.

5. Commas have many purposes, but they are *not* primarily for verbal pauses. Use them wisely.

6. FANBOYS: for, and, nor, but, or, yet, so. These are coordinating conjunctions, and you can continue to string together clauses of a sentence with them after a comma.

7. Do not join independent clauses with a comma. You can join them with a semicolon—or make a new sentence after a period, or use a FANBOY.

8. Parentheses can be used (like these ones) to add supplementary ideas not essential to the sentence. So can dashes—like this one.

9. Make sure your subjects and your verbs agree.

What is a sentence? A sentence is merely one thought expressed in a set of words. It begins with a capital letter and it ends with a period (or in the case of a question, a question mark). It generally contains a **subject** and **verb**, but sometimes those are implied and not made obvious. The sentence is the basic unit of writing. And even the most complex or substantial writing is never more than a collection of sentences, well-crafted and carefully revised.

Sentences have parts or **clauses**. If the clause can stand alone as its own sentence, we call it an **independent clause**. If it cannot stand alone, we call it a **dependent clause**. (There are more complex subdivisions of clause types—restrictive, for example—but for now this main division should suffice.)

Subjects and Verbs and Objects

The grammatical subject is **not** the *topic* of a sentence. The subject is the thing (sometimes a person) that controls the verb. The subject is often the thing doing something or acting on something. The object is the thing having something done to it. That's confusing, yes, but all confusing things are made up of smaller, less-confusing parts. Let's examine it with a few examples.

Clear, declarative writing often follows this formula: **subject + verb + object**. This formula has its limits, yes, but keeping it in mind as a basic format for sentences means you won't veer too far off course. Here is the basic version of a declarative sentence in action, using the subject + verb + object formula:

Radhika completed her work.

Radhika	**completed**	**her work.**
subject	verb	object

Steven opened the door.

Steven	**opened**	**the door.**
subject	verb	object

Simple? Yes, and this form is not always suited to academic writing. But where you can, use it. The reader will thank you.

Here are a few more worked examples of this clear, declarative form.

Wealth inequality affects everyone.

"Wealth inequality" is the subject here. "Affects" is the verb. "Everyone" is the object.

Or consider the earlier quotation from Pinker: "**I love style manuals**" (*Sense of Style* 1). Clear and simple and direct. And it also follows the formula above.

Here's a more complex example from the *Harvard Gazette*: "Too many leaders and influencers, including politicians, journalists, intellectuals, and academics, surrender to the cognitive bias of assessing the world through anecdotes and images rather than data and facts" (Pinker, "One Thing").

Yes, more complex, but ultimately subjects are doing something: <u>Too many leaders and influencers</u> (the subjects) <u>surrender</u> (the verb) to the <u>cognitive bias</u>. It's a beautiful sentence and a good example of scholarly writing that is both plain and rich. We would do well to keep this form in mind when writing, use it as a default setting, and adjust when needed.

Capitalization Rules

Capital letters go in *only* a few places.

1. Every sentence begins with a capital letter.
2. All proper nouns get them, too.

    Nouns are generally persons, places, and things.
    Common nouns are everyday versions: car, boat, school, person.
    Proper nouns are specific versions: Porsche, *RMS Titanic*, University of Toronto, James.

Advanced Maneuvers

In some style guides, including APA, you should capitalize the first word after a colon if it is a complete sentence. For example,

> It's been raining all night: **The** garden is flooded.

> (That said, this is a gray area, and other style guides disagree. In MLA, for example, we don't use capital letters after colons.)

What about titles? Capitalize the first and last words, always. Capitalize all other words, too, except articles (a, an, the), coordinating conjunctions (but, and), and prepositions (on, in).[1]

Three title examples:

> *A Tale of Two Cities*; *On Golden Pond*; *The Sense of Style*

Punctuation Rules

At times, many aspects of writing clearly can seem without much rule or reason. It can sound, if we're not listening closely, as if writing teachers are simply making up rules for their own sake. But if we listen carefully, and pay attention to the challenge of writing clearly, with the reader in mind, we start to understand that these small-but-important details may make the difference between being understood by your readers and merely frustrating them. Pinker puts it well: "Literate readers rely on punctuation to guide them through a sentence, and mastering the basics is a nonnegotiable requirement for anyone who writes" (*Sense of Style* 121).

---

1   See, for example, the APA guidance (Lee).

Punctuation Mark	Appearance	Purpose
Period	•	Full stop. The red traffic light of the writing world.
Comma	,	Separates clauses in a sentence and is used in lists.
Colon	:	Begins a list, or used for emphasis in a sentence.
Semicolon	;	Joins two independent clauses, while indicating that they are thematically linked. Can also be used within lists.
Quotation Marks	" "	Indicates that you have taken another writer's words verbatim. In North America, quotation marks are double and always go outside the punctuation mark—they act as fences and keep the punctuation marks in.
Apostrophe	'	Generally used in two ways: to show possession and to indicate a contraction.

Punctuation Mark	Appearance	Purpose
Dash	—	A very useful mark often used to signal an additional thought—either at the end of a sentence or in the middle.
Parentheses	( )	Like a dash, a very useful mark often used to signal an additional thought—either at the end of a sentence or in the middle.

Full Stop: The Period

All sentences must end with a period. They are the red light of the punctuation world. There is a simple clarity for the reader, an ease of digestion if you have nice, clear, full stops. Yes, you can have lots of long sentences, and they can still be technically correct, but too many long sentences can exhaust the reader. When working to understand a sentence, our brains have to hold a lot of details in working memory. A period allows us as readers to move on and free up some processing power to understand what comes next.

Commas

There are few pieces of punctuation as misunderstood as the comma. I get frustrated when intelligent people tell young writers things like, "Just put a comma wherever you think the reader needs a break, or where you want to take a breath." Commas have rules, and the rules help the reader understand your writing.

There are probably more than a dozen comma rules, and they all have their place—but that place might not be in this short book. I recommend reading further in resources listed in Appendix C. But the list below is likely the short-but-relevant list of rules to follow.

Major Comma Uses

- **Before a FANBOY to extend a sentence**
  We went to the store, and when we were there we bought candy.
- **After a dependent phrase or clause that starts a sentence**
  When they are well fed, students are eager and excited to learn.
- **In a list**
  We had three aims that day: victory, fun, and friendship.

A note on the serial or Oxford comma: there is some dispute on whether or not to use a comma before "and" in a list like this:

We had three aims that day: victory, fun, and friendship. (Oxford comma)

We had three aims that day: victory, fun and friendship. (Not Oxford comma)

Some style guides say you should use the extra comma, while others say you shouldn't. I see no compelling reason why a writer would avoid the Oxford comma in most cases. You certainly don't want the absurdity of thanking for their inspiration your parents, Mahatma Gandhi and Nelson Mandela (rather than your parents, Mahatma Gandhi, and

Nelson Mandela). But you do want to think carefully about the two possible meanings of a sentence such as this:

We should consult those most knowledgeable on the subject, our Accounts Department and our sales team.

We should consult those most knowledgeable on the subject, our Accounts Department, and our sales team.

My advice: unless doing so would clearly create confusion or change your intended meaning, use the Oxford comma.

Colons

A colon can do a few things:

1.   Colons can begin a list

     I had three things in mind: baseball, basketball, and hockey.
     (... But not when it would be unnatural.
     E.g., "I excel at: baseball, basketball, and hockey.")

2.   They can act as a mark of emphasis.

     Students who don't do their readings have a predictable experience: failure.

Semicolons

Like periods, semicolons separate independent clauses,[1] but as they do so they indicate that the clauses are thematically linked.

Examples:

I didn't like the movie; it was too long.

It's difficult to imagine the opposition winning the upcoming elections; the government remains extremely popular.

Semicolons can also act as divisions in a complex list.

Example:

The medieval school had many parts: a lecture hall, where the boring professors droned on; a field, where the ritual bonfires were held; and a dungeon, used to imprison the wayward boys.

(In this case, the semicolons allow the use of commas between items in a list.)

Common Punctuation Errors to Avoid

Comma Splice

A comma splice occurs when you use a comma where a period or semicolon is needed. As Strunk said back in 1918, "Do not join

---

1   Reminder: an independent clause is a part of a sentence that could stand alone as its own sentence.

independent clauses by a comma." This is a case where knowing a little bit about clauses is essential if we are to write clearly.

Example:

I didn't like the movie, it was too long.

Why is this a comma splice? Both halves could stand alone as their own sentence, so we know they are independent clauses. Joining them with a comma is confusing to the reader.

There are options to fix the comma splice:

I didn't like the movie. It was too long.
(Add a period and start a new sentence.)

I didn't like the movie; it was too long.
(Replace the comma with a semicolon.)

I didn't like the movie because it was too long.
(Replace the comma with a coordinating conjunction.)

Fused Sentences

A fused sentence occurs when we merge two sentences together—two independent clauses without any punctuation between them. As with most errors in writing, the fused sentence forces the reader to work hard to understand your meaning.

Example:

I went to the store it was out of potato chips. (Fused)

There are options to fix the fused sentence:

I went to the store; it was out of potato chips.
(Semicolons join independent clauses.)

I went to the store, but it was out of potato chips.
(Commas plus FANBOYS fix fused sentences.)

I went to the store. It was out of potato chips.
(If you want a full stop between the independent clauses,
use a period.)

Rules Governing Possession

Some things "possess" other things. A cat has fur, a car has wheels,
and you have essays. The rules governing possessives are very easy
to learn, but it's also easy to become confused in the heat of writing.

Singular Possessive: Singular Noun + 's

Examples:

The cat's fur shone, the car's wheels spun, and Serena's
essay was complete.
(In these cases, we merely take the noun and add an apostrophe and an S.)

Plural Possessive: Plural Noun + '

Examples:

All the students' course fees were unpaid, and all the administrators' brows were furrowed in despair.

**(In these cases, because the plural noun ends in an S, we
merely add an apostrophe at the end.)**

What about Singular Nouns That End in an S?

Style guides differ on this question, but I see no reason to violate
the basic rule.

Examples:

James's car was rusty.
**(If we wrote, as some style guides suggest, James' car, we
are really saying there are multiple people named "Jame."
Why not avoid the confusion and merely write James's and
follow the rule?)**

Apostrophe Use

Be careful, though: English being the marvel that it is, apostrophes
can be used to indicate a contraction, not just to show possession.

Do not = don't   **Cannot = can't**

The English language can be frustrating, though. Above we learned
that the apostrophe was used to indicate possession ("Sarah's mind
was nimble"). One of the most common errors young writers con-
front involves a confusion between it's and its. Because in this case,
the rule above is reversed.

It's = contraction of it is   **Its = possessive**

Examples:

> The car spun **its** wheels. (Possessive)
> **It's** such a nice day today. (Contraction)

CHAPTER 16

Advanced Style Maneuvers

Moving Beyond the Elementary

THOUGH THE BASIC RULES OF COMPOSITION ARE A GOOD start, they are only that.

Paragraph Structure

Even writers possessed of subtlety use something like the following format when writing paragraphs: paragraphs have one main idea, they begin with a topic sentence, they move on to write sentences that develop, extend, and complexify ideas, and they finish the paragraph with some concluding remark—and perhaps a transition to the next idea.

This structure is not arbitrary. Our brains do well when they are prepared for what will come next, which is what topic sentences do. (Think of a preview of a film or an overture of a symphony; it helps to know what to expect.) The middle section of the paragraph allows you to explore that topic in depth: look for ways to mix the summary of evidence with your own commentary, and place voices of scholars in conversation explicitly. And then conclude to remind the reader of what the major significance of the paragraph is, and how it fits into the overall story of your argument.

One common fault of first drafts: a string of underdeveloped paragraphs. To solve the dilemma of the weak paragraph, you have a few options:

1. Build it up! More fully develop each paragraph with greater evidence, elaboration, or commentary. Highlight more fully what this paragraph says and how.
2. Merge it! Bring similar paragraphs together. When we have a string of undeveloped paragraphs, typically a few of them often fit together and in our haste we needlessly separated them. Join a few and smooth out the transitions between ideas.
3. Cut it! Omit the weak paragraph. Sometimes we write paragraphs imagining we have something good to say, and it turns out we don't. Cut the weak writing and leave space for the richer ideas to thrive.

Artful Introductions and Conclusions

Introductory paragraphs are essential in joining the academic conversation, and they should be attended to carefully. Commonly, academic papers make some reference to the previous research on the topic, and then narrow to the thesis statement, which is frequently the last sentence of the introduction. Consider this example, taken from a paper written by two Nobel-Prize-winning scholars:

Recent research has begun to distinguish two aspects of subjective well-being. Emotional well-being refers to the emotional quality of an individual's everyday experience—the frequency and intensity of experiences of joy, stress, sadness, anger, and affection that make one's life pleasant or unpleasant. Life evaluation refers to the thoughts that people have about their life when they think about it. We raise the question of whether money buys happiness, separately for these two aspects of well-being. We report an analysis of more than 450,000 responses to the Gallup-Healthways Well-Being Index, a daily survey of 1,000 US residents conducted by the Gallup Organization. We find that ... income and education are more closely related to life evaluation, but health, care giving, loneliness, and smoking are relatively stronger predictors of daily emotions. When plotted against log income, life evaluation rises steadily. Emotional well-being also rises with log income, but there is no further progress beyond an annual income of ~$75,000. Low income exacerbates the emotional pain associated with such misfortunes as divorce, ill health, and being alone. We conclude that high income buys life satisfaction but not happiness, and that low income is associated both with low life evaluation and low emotional well-being. (Kahneman and Deaton)[1]

The strength of this paragraph is that it indicates clearly where the authors are taking us, what our journey will involve, and why. The

---

1   This (slightly shortened) paragraph is the abstract with which Kahneman and Deaton open their article. Conventions differ in different academic disciplines; in several, the abstract performs essentially the same function that the opening paragraph of the "essay proper" performs in others.

introduction begins with referencing recent research, which bumps up against an age-old question, and then narrows to the authors' central argument presented in the final sentence.

The second thing all readers need is some reason to find this topic interesting. Why does it matter? What is the significance of the question at hand? The authors above do this expertly with a reference to things of obvious interest to us all ("The frequency and intensity of experiences of joy, stress, sadness, anger, and affection that make one's life pleasant or unpleasant"). You might do so with a reference to, for example, monetary issues (is it costly?), moral dimensions (is there something unfair about the thing you're writing about?), the scope and scale of the issue (how many people does this question affect?), or anything else that will convince your reader that their attention on your paper is well spent.

One consideration: many writers find they are not able to write a good introduction until they have written a good draft of their paper. After all, if the introduction prepares the reader for what comes next, and you want the reader to understand the writer's argument in a thorough and nuanced way, it might not be possible to write the introduction until you know what that argument looks like. So feel free to write the introduction after you have written the body of your paper. Doing so may make for a better introduction.

Remember: A finished paper looks like it was written in order, word by word. The process is often much messier than that ideal.

Conclusions have the need to do more than simply repeat your main points. Yes, summarize as necessary; the reader will benefit from being reminded of some key ideas. But you should go beyond this most basic step.

What else should a writer do in the conclusion besides summarize? While there are many ways to go here, the most fruitful way may be to extend your argument by considering the implications and consequences of your ideas. If we accept what you've told us, if your argument rings true, *how would we or the world be different?*

Let's say that, using the example of the introduction above, we find that it has been determined that happiness (or "emotional well-being") rises with income, but only to a level of approximately $75,000 a year, after which it plateaus. If that is the case, in our conclusion, we might extend our argument in the final paragraph by

1. Considering policy issues: Should we work to increase people's happiness through economic prosperity?
2. Considering moral issues: Is it fair that those earning more than $75,000 a year have a special subjective well-being advantage? Should we, as a society, enact different tax policies to redistribute income?[1]
3. By suggesting future research: Is the concept of "happiness" and the various survey tools used to measure it well understood? If not, what more work needs to be done?
4. By suggesting changes in social norms: Should we emphasize wealth creation in the way we raise young people?

---

1 Kahneman and Deaton themselves provide a somewhat cautiously worded commentary on possible policy implications in the final paragraph of the "Discussion" section at the end of the article:

Not everyone will agree that enhancing the happiness experienced by those who are already quite happy is a legitimate policy objective. The policy goal of reducing suffering is likely to raise fewer objections, and measures of emotional pain may be useful for that purpose. This topic merits serious debate. (16492)

Generally speaking, at some point in your conclusion, you want to extend your thinking to explore kinds of "now what?" questions. You need not come to firm and unyielding policy recommendations (intellectual humility is valuable), but your best provisional conclusion should suggest new ways of looking at things, or ways we might continue to explore this question in future. You have added in a small way to the academic conversation, and if you are right—if your evidence is compelling and well-used, if you have done the best possible job in answering your initial research question—the world should be slightly different knowing what we know now from your work. Spell it out to the reader in your conclusion.

Avoid Needless Personalization—Can I Use "I"?

Young writers often wonder if they can use "I" in their writing. The answer is: of course! There are many, many good reasons to use personal pronouns in writing. For example, to keep sentences in the active voice when writing scientific studies: "For this study, we surveyed 62,451 Americans about their voting preferences." To avoid personal pronouns often means to torture your sentences: "The present study utilized a survey method…." Memoirs, of course, require the personal pronoun.

But beware: personal pronouns very often add needless clutter and serve to weaken your writing. We often use personal pronouns conversationally in our writing, as in the following sentence:

> "I believe that the evidence shows rent control legislation reduces the availability of apartments to rent." (Worse)

> "~~I believe that~~ The evidence shows rent control legislation reduces the availability of apartments to rent." (Better)

The second sentence is far stronger: it is clearer, more direct; it is less fuzzy ("belief" isn't really a relevant factor in academic writing); and the reader already knows it's you who is writing.

A good general rule: unless you as the writer or researcher are integral to the sentence, there is no need to use a personal pronoun.

> **Rule of Thumb:** Unless they are essential to the meaning, personal pronouns are either distracting or add unnecessary words, weakening your claim and the clarity of your writing.

Vocabulary: Simple and Direct

When we want to seem impressive, we can get ourselves into trouble. In this case, when we want to seem smart, we are tempted to use words too complex for the purpose. This desire for simplicity should not be taken to imply that complexity is our enemy: far from it. But choosing the simplest word is usually the best way to convey the clearest meaning. Simple, plain, direct: these should be our goals. Here's an example, from a book by Margaret MacMillan, an acclaimed Oxford University historian who has specialized in the study of war and diplomacy:

> Like Wilson, [Franklin Delano Roosevelt] was elected on a platform that focused on pressing domestic issues, and like his predecessor, he would have preferred to concentrate on problems at home and, where necessary, deal with the United States' immediate neighbors, but the great and ominous changes happening in the wider world in the 1930s obliged him to take an ever-increasing interest in developments abroad. For much of the decade, his foreign policy evolved

by fits and starts. It is easy to criticize many of his actions, such as his decision, in 1933, apparently on a whim, to op- pose an attempt to stabilize international exchange rates.... His many critics then and now believe that he could have done much more during the 1930s to rally the democracies to oppose the rise of the dictatorships. Yet if he had struck out too forcefully, he might well have stimulated isolationist sentiments in the American population and, crucially, lost the votes of isolationists in Congress.... Like the sailor he was, he knew he was sailing in treacherous waters and that shipwreck was likely at any time. (60–61)

Not surprisingly, MacMillan uses a good many abstract nouns and multisyllabic words; you can't write about diplomatic history and international exchange rates while using only one-syllable words familiar to any grade schooler. But look at the sorts of phrases she uses when real choice is open to her. She chooses *in the wider world* rather than *in the international community*; she chooses *by fits and starts* rather than *erratically and unpredictably*; she chooses *on a whim* rather than *without any substantial degree of forethought*; she chooses *then and now* rather than *both in his own era and in the twenty-first cen- tury*. She chooses too to include an extended metaphor, using a suc- cession of simple, concrete nouns—*sailor, waters, shipwreck*—that are easily understood by any reader. Many students—and not a few professors—have been persuaded that it is better in an academic context to write *without any substantial degree of forethought* than it is to write *on a whim*. They're wrong.

Rule 11[1]—(Usually) Phrase in the Active voice

You might recall that earlier in the book I mentioned that I learned of "**passive voice**" when I got to university. Learning of it was one of my first inklings that I wasn't as good a writer as I wanted to be. I hadn't known what it was and had been committing this error all along, apparently.

But what is it? The simplest way to understand the passive voice is through example.

Active voice	Vladimir hit the ball.
Passive voice	The ball was hit by Vladimir.
Active voice	Deborah read the book.
Passive voice	The book was read by Deborah.
Active voice	At the conference, many scientists noted the rise in global temperatures.
Passive Voice	At the conference, the rise in global temperatures was noted by many scientists.

All of the active sentences have fewer words; all are clear and direct. These examples teach us a few important lessons.

1. Passive voice tends to emphasize the object.
2. Passive voice tends to add words.

---

1   In a few places, this text refers to the original rules from the classic writing guide, *Elements of Style*. While the numbers of the rules have changed over the years, the essence remains. See the list of the original rules here: https://www.bartleby.com/141/.

3. Passive voice often ends up requiring the use of "was/were."

4. Passive voice is generally more awkward and confusing to the reader—but not always!

Here's a good example of how the use of passive voice can tire out the reader: "It was recorded by Platt that 25 million people were licensed drivers. It was also shown that around 30 per cent of Canadians commute to work in a car, truck or van daily." The give-away is the succession of "was" constructions. It is needlessly passive. Here it is reworded in the active voice. "Platt found that 25 million Canadians have a driver's license, and 30% commute to work in a car, truck, or van daily."

Remember: Excessive passive voice often leads to long and tortured sentences. Academic writing can and should be clear and direct. Don't be seduced by the notion that formal writing needs to be hard to understand.

My suggestion: strive for simple and direct active constructions, generally subject + verb + object. That said, there are many instances where the passive voice may make more sense. For example, where you want to emphasize the object, using the passive voice makes sense. Imagine we were writing a book on World War II. Our first sentence could be either of the next two sentences:

The German army invaded Poland on September 1, 1939. (Active)

Poland **was invaded by** the German army on September 1, 1939. (Passive)

If you are writing a book about Poland, the passive construction makes sense.

Exceptions to rules like this always exist. Earlier in the book, I quoted from the Declaration of Independence. Many writers have noticed that this glorious piece of text has many passive constructions: "We hold these truths to be self-evident, that all men are created equal, that they are endowed by their Creator with certain unalienable Rights, that among these are Life, Liberty and the pursuit of Happiness" (Poser). Phrasing those sentences in the active voice would not improve it.

Rule 12—Generally, Phrase in the Positive Form

Clear writing requires clear, declarative sentences where the writer tells the reader something. Phrase in the positive form—to say what is rather than what is not.[1]

Negative Form	Positive Form
Don't phrase in the negative form ...	Phrase in the positive ...
Not getting enough sleep is often overlooked as a non-serious and non-harmful issue, but ...	Sleep deprivation is misunderstood as benign or trivial ...

---

1   One can write in the positive form about "negative" things. You could say for example that "this food tastes terrible," which is in the positive form.

As these examples show, writing a string of negative phrases can force your reader to struggle through needless words.

Of course, there are good reasons to phrase in the negative. You might seek to draw attention to the negative, or drop in variety to a string of tiresome and repetitive phrasings. Some elegant and powerful phrasings use the negative form. For example, Strunk did so in his "Omit Needless Words" paragraph in order to draw a contrast: "This requires not that the writer make all his sentences short, or that he avoid all detail and treat his subjects only in outline, but that every word tell."

Yes, this rule can be artfully broken. But in general, phrase in the positive form.

Unclear Antecedents—Which That Is This?

Be careful when using "that" or "this"—their misuse can be confusing. Here's an example provided by Letitia Henville in *University Affairs* magazine:

> The multitude of factors that contribute to Vancouver's high youth homelessness rate makes it difficult for healthcare providers to provide appropriate care to young, vulnerable women. This exacerbates the impact of the opioid crisis.

As Henville points out, the writer in the passage above does not make clear in the sentence what "this" refers to; the reader is forced to return to the previous sentences to try to figure it out. She writes, "What specifically exacerbates the impact of the opioid crisis? Is it the lack of appropriate care for young, vulnerable women? The difficulties of healthcare providers in this context? The high homelessness rate? The multitude of factors that contribute to this high rate?

Or some combination of all of these?" The writer has to make the meaning plain.

The solution to this sort of problem is actually easy: give the reader something after "this" that helps clarify. In this case, Henville suggests we might write: "This inconsistent care exacerbates the impact of the opioid crisis." I agree. Without something after "this," readers are forced back into the paragraph to do some detective work.

Sometimes we fall into a curse-of-knowledge trap that's even deeper and more confusing to the reader. Consider this example: "Sea levels are rising, habitat is being destroyed, and the climate is changing. This means that governments urgently need to change their policies." To *what* is "This" referring? Again, the reader has to return to the previous sentences and make some guesses. Whenever you see "this" or "that" stranded alone without a noun in this way, add a little something. In this case, consider: "This unprecedented threat to ecosystems means that governments urgently need to change their policies." Here's another example:

> When taking up homework, smart teachers call on students randomly. No one knew who would be called on next; that increases the number of kids who are likely to be on task and thinking about the question.

> When taking up homework, smart teachers call on students randomly. No one knew who would be called on next; that uncertainty increases the number of kids who are likely to be on task and thinking about the question.

When you notice you have written a "that" or "this," double check that your reader has enough information in the sentence to understand what you refer to. Generally, err on the side of including a word or two after "that" or "this" to give the reader effortless clarity.

Omit Needless Words

No one could explain this better than William Strunk:

> Vigorous writing is concise. A sentence should contain no unnecessary words, a paragraph no unnecessary sentences, for the same reason that a drawing should have no unnecessary lines and a machine no unnecessary parts. This requires not that the writer make all his sentences short, or that he avoid all detail and treat his subjects only in outline, but that every word tell.

Here are a few stock phrases often associated with wordiness:

- as you know, as we all know
- at the present time
- in close proximity to
- due to the fact that
- from my point of view, according to my point of view
- it is interesting to note that

But omitting needless words is not just a matter of avoiding wordy stock phrases. It's also a matter of rephrasing to make your sentences shorter and more direct. Words such as *aspect* and *factor* and *situation*—as well as *there is/there are* sentence structures—are worth paying particular attention to. Here are two examples:

One of the aspects of this topic that deserves attention is the degree to which people in low-income situations suffer disproportionately during times of economic slowdown.

Not everyone suffers equally during recessions; typically, low-income people suffer more.

There were many factors involved in the undermining of the level of popularity of the government over the course of the following five years.

The government's popularity fell over the next five years, for a number of reasons.

Beware the Word "Proves"!

There was no one more guilty than I was as a young writer of using overly strong language in my writing. I probably couldn't bear to re-read some of it. I seem to remember that everything was severe.

Remember: Great academic writing can be modest. Your claim should not be grander than the evidence presented.

You can avoid the pitfall I fell into. How? Ensure your conclusions are rooted in the evidence and be alive to the notion that most issues are complex and that few answers are definitive. Then take care to phrase your writing with that awareness. In almost no academic study is a complex real-world question proven one way or another. Remember to survey the landscape of the issue; build in counter-arguments and complexity by considering, in explicit ways, the limits of your evidence, and the possible objections a thoughtful intellectual opponent might make. In most cases, it is better to write "This evidence strongly suggests," rather than "This evidence proves," better to write "The information available to us now seems to indicate that earlier generations of scholars were mistaken," rather than "the information presented in this paper shows without a doubt that earlier generations of scholars were mistaken." Always qualify your conclusions where appropriate. Write "in most cases." Write "very likely." Be very wary of writing "proves."

CHAPTER 17

Sharing with an Audience

What Story Do I Want to Tell?
A Quick Guide to Academic Presentations

SEEN ONE WAY, WHAT WE ARE DOING WHEN WE PRESENT our academic findings is describing the world as we understand it. If we have performed research, we have learned something new—lots of new things, really—and we are now sharing it with the world.

But in a more fundamental way, we aren't just reporting facts: we are telling a story. Sometimes students turn away from the metaphor of a story in academic work—indeed, most academics shy away from that word, too. The word "story" suggests fiction, and research is rooted in truth. But consider any fictional story: for it to capture the reader, it needs to be structured carefully, it needs to be worded with an ear to compel, and, perhaps most importantly, a story needs to tell itself by choosing carefully what details to include and which to omit.

Remember: While the particulars of the format are different, delivering an academic presentation is fundamentally similar to writing; your audience requires much the same thing to follow along and understand your work.

Your presentation should have a beginning, a middle, and an end. You should choose your words carefully, sharing with the audience only the most relevant details, drawing out the most important conclusions, selecting and highlighting only the most important evidence—and doing so with a storyteller's ear.

How Should I Tell the Story of My Research?

Of course, there is no one correct way to present your academic research. Gifted presenters often use a variety of approaches, and there couldn't possibly be only one way to present. But when we're learning any new task, models are helpful. So here is one. In general, the most interesting academic presentations, like most academic papers, have something like the following structure:

1. **A brief description of the topic**
    In two or three sentences, what's the presentation about? *Strive for clarity and brevity in the opening.* In two simple and clear sentences, what is your work about?

2. **A section suggesting why the audience might care**
    Spend a slide or so on establishing why this matters, who it affects, and the importance of the topic at hand. As in your writing, consider economic, moral, or political dimensions, as a start.

3. **A clear statement of your argument**
   Clearly state your main point to the audience as clearly as possible. Perhaps give it its own slide. Return to it, both in slides and in words. You want the audience, if asked, to be able to recount your main point back to you at the end of the presentation.

4. **Clearly defined reasons, with sufficient evidence (but no more!), to persuade the audience**
   You will likely have to leave out large portions of your written work and emphasize only what matters. Brains that are listening do not have the same attention span as brains that are reading.

5. **A consideration of the limits of your ideas—and alternative hypotheses**
   Your presentation needs to find ways to consider alternative explanations of the evidence, the limitations of your ideas and analysis, and general critiques of your own work. Act as a reasonable critic of your own work.

6. **Conclusion—where you consider the consequences of your ideas**
   Now that we know what you learned, what is the value of the conclusions? Why do they matter?

As in all matters of joining the academic conversation, your presentation is an opportunity for you to communicate with others, share with them what you have learned, and in a small way, improve the human condition. That is not an overstatement: all progress comes when people learn new things and share them with an audience in some form or other. That is all—and what an "all"!—you're doing when you present your work.

Presentation Performance

Whether we like it or not, our ideas are not judged only by their intellectual merits, but also by the way we deliver them. We all know this instinctively. When we try to follow a "bad" speaker, we struggle, we feel frustrated, or maybe worst of all, our boredom forces us to disregard the speaker entirely.

The good news: you need not be extraordinary in your speaking skills to capture an audience and communicate effectively. There are only so many superhuman performers—most very good speakers are entirely ordinary in their talents. You can be compelling and engaging by attending to a few simple concepts. Speaking effectively is a skill, and like all skills, it can be practiced and learned.

Here are some general techniques to follow when speaking in front of an audience. As always, begin with what the audience needs.

What Do Listening Brains Need?

1. **Organized ideas are easier to follow**. Structure your talk carefully, telegraph to your audience what that structure is, and remind them of key points as you go along. Let's make an analogy to reading: when you read a challenging passage, you will notice that you stop and start a bit, return to previous sentences, think to yourself, and generally take your time to understand the writer's direction. When listening, we have no such luxury. An old adage is "Tell them what you're going to say, say it, then tell them what you just told them." While a cliché, it's not too far off.

Tip: Listen to an old but famous speech—many can be found on YouTube. Note how slowly the speakers proceed, and how many pauses there are. You might be amazed.

2. **Listening brains need pauses.** Many excellent speakers would be even better if they made judicious use of pauses. Empty space has the effect of sharpening the attention of your audience. During the next conversation you have, pause without filling the silence with any "um"s or "aahs"s for a full *four seconds* between two sentences. See how dramatically the other person focuses on you.

3. **Avoid simply reading the screen, but do highlight key ideas.** It can feel reassuring to simply read the words you've put on the slide. It is familiar—we can all read, and it is one way to ensure the presentation passes quickly. But our goal isn't just to run through the presentation and sit down: it is to memorably convey the substance of our research. To do so, we need to take care to highlight the most important evidence and—even more crucial— clearly communicate the underlying meaning of our work to the audience. Always ask yourself: What matters here, and how can I stress that to the audience?

4. **Engaging voices have enthusiasm and some variety in tone.** No one expects you to perform as well as the best TED Talk speakers. Some of these performances have inspired millions of people, and some of those speakers are gifted presenters who have spent decades practicing the skills involved in capturing an audience. You do not need to be such a god. But simply because you might not have the gift of a stage persona that automatically engages

your audience doesn't mean you give up trying. The basics: use vocal variation, energy, and enthusiasm. You are selling ideas here. Keep your passion up, and others will come along for the ride.

5. **Stress relevance whenever possible**. Brains are relevance-seeking machines. Listeners need to know the answer to "Why does this matter? What does this mean?" Make these considerations a part of your plan to reach the audience. Remember: they don't yet know what you know.

6. **Know your material**. This rule applies to the specifics of your argument, of course: know what you are saying (and why) with perfect clarity. But as well, it applies to the need to rehearse. Speakers who are unfamiliar with their material will inevitably turn off their audience. We need to think the people we're listening to have credibility or else our brains decide to do something else with their attention.

The Use of Notes

Great speakers use notes. Some great speakers can work from memory, but the vast majority have notes (or, in the modern world, use a teleprompter). New Zealand's charismatic Prime Minister Jacinda Ardern—named "the world's most eloquent leader" in 2020[1]—uses notes when she delivers a speech. Abraham Lincoln delivered the Gettysburg Address holding the speech. The question is not, "can I

---

1   See "'Compassionate': Jacinda Ardern Ranked World's Most Eloquent Leader." *New Zealand Herald*, 30 July 2020, https://www.nzherald.co.nz/nz/compassionate-jacinda-ardern-ranked-worlds-most-eloquent-leader/EXLN2TDYM24C3TZDQWETWLYOTU/.

use notes?" Because, yes, you certainly can use notes—*and I suggest doing so!* The question is, "How can I use notes in ways that ensure I sound like a human, speaking to an audience of humans?" Use notes sparingly for key data and facts that no one could be expected to memorize. Used well, notes are a critical support for the best speakers.

But one sin to be avoided: never read the entire presentation. At this point in your academic career, such a performance will not really suffice. You need to present what you have to say like a human speaking to a room of humans. There is a comfort, perhaps, in just reading, in hiding yourself from the eyes of the audience and retreating into your prepared speech. If our goal is to make our audience understand the world as we do, there is no way to do it without looking them in the face.

CHAPTER 18

Slide Design

Showing AND Telling

GIVEN THE SHORT TIME YOU HAVE TO BE HEARD, *HOW* YOU deliver your message can sometimes be at least as important as the *substance* of it.

Visuals! Elephants in the Room

Imagine you are a management consultant and you are about to give a presentation to a room of clients. You want to convince them of something—say, that they aren't engaging in the most profitable business practices, or there are glaring errors in their approach to marketing their products. You could start by saying those things directly, and there is good reason to do so: being clear is a virtue. But when telling a story via slide deck, it helps to emphasize the visuals.

Perhaps you begin, as many management consultants do,[1] with a slide like the one below. If you were an audience member, what might you think looking at this slide? You might be puzzled—you might whisper something to the person next to you: "What's that all about?" The important thing: you would be focused on the image, and primed to listen to what the speaker was about to say.

---

1   This is a common enough tactic that a quick Google search of "Elephant in the room slides" produces many, many results—often self-assured management types standing in a room with an elephant. Thanks to Anthony Campbell for letting me know about this.

The answer to what's going on here: **this is the elephant in the room**. (According to the *Cambridge Dictionary*: "If you say there is an elephant in the room, you mean that there is an obvious problem or difficult situation that people do not want to talk about.") This kind of highly memorable, engaging idea is sometimes called "sticky"[1]—an idea that *captivates* rather than merely *informs*. Setting the threshold of success at sticky ideas is ambitious but also admirable. While you might not be as playful as the elephant in the room example above, we can set as our goal a slide design that does more than simply present data or have large chunks of text. Aim for at least clear, and see if you can add in sticky, too.

Basic Techniques of Slide Clarity

1. **Have a focus or intention for each slide.**[2] What is the purpose of the slide? How will you communicate that to the audience? Omit unnecessary or distracting information. Be sure to create a clear, powerful, and distinct message on every slide, and seek feedback to understand if others see it as you do.
2. **Present key information on its own slide**. Don't bury the most important material in a large list of bullet points. Have large text on its own slide to emphasize key ideas. If you have an argument, say it on its own slide. Say it clearly. Here is an effective and simple slide from a recent student presentation:

---

1   See, for example, Heath and Heath, the originators of much of this thinking.
2   Thank you to Jack De Aragon, Joey Lisser, Sebastian Raman, and Joseph Vretenar for the images in this section.

Our Solution: Page 15

Create a New Government Organization, Focusing Solely on The Regulation of Data Mining

3. **Font size should be big**. You should generally not go below 24-pt font for something you want anyone to read easily.

4. **Use data well**. Numbers and graphs can be exceptionally good at telling a story, but you need to ensure that the data isn't just a jumble of numbers. How? If you want to point out that 54 per cent of all statistics are made up on the spot, why not have just the number 54 per cent at 60-pt font? That's a sticky slide design. If you want to use a graph, fine—but before doing so you should ask yourself if your audience might struggle to understand its meaning. If so, how could you simplify it so as to highlight only the key features and figures?

5. **Consider the visual layout of text and ideas**. Avoid a thoughtless mess of material on the screen. Shape the text and ideas as carefully as possible for your purpose. Again, ask yourself: What is the intention of this particular slide—and how can I compose a thoughtful layout to achieve that intention? For example, when comparing

various conclusions or solutions, it might be appropriate
to use a table like this:

Strategic Solutions:				Page 14
Solutions	**Privacy**	**Corporate Impact**	**Costs**	**Decision**
Ban Data Mining	+	✕	✕	✕
Make No Changes	✕	+	+	✕
Develop Data-Protecting Technology	+	+	+	✕
Nationalize Big Tech	+	✕	✕	✕
Draft Updated Laws	+	+	+	+
Data Mining Regulation Agency	+	+	+	+

Chosen Solutions

This table is a lot of text, true—but speaking well while
standing beside it while highlighting its central meaning
may be an efficient way to assess competing ideas within
a presentation. Note the use of shading and shapes.
Symbols can speak well on their own.

6. **End credits**. It is a good idea to include a slide at the end
   with relevant citations. (If this presentation comes after
   having written an academic paper, it should be easy to
   merely copy and paste the citations from the reference
   list of your paper into your slide.) It is good practice to be
   transparent with your evidence so that others may explore
   your sources.[1]

---

1   One interesting idea: make a Google Doc with all your citations in there, and
any supplemental information, and link that Doc to a QR code which you leave up
on the screen at the end.

Slide Design Sins to Avoid

As with most complex tasks, we often succeed by avoiding the worst sins rather than being a superhero. Here are some pitfalls of less-than-good slide designs:

1. **Too much text**. Avoid confusing your slides with your notes. Don't simply copy what you want to say onto the slides—if you force your audience to read too much, they won't listen—and might just disengage entirely. (Also, see above: small text is poison for attention spans!)

2. **Poor contrast between elements**. Ensure that your backgrounds don't outshine the text. Ensure that the font used has the right color contrast with other elements. Just because lime green text on a gray background looks bright on your laptop, that doesn't mean it will look great on a screen.

3. **Too many slides**. Death by PowerPoint is a real threat here. In a 10-minute presentation, more than 10 slides is likely a recipe for audience exhaustion.

4. **A string of undifferentiated bullet points**. Remember: you are telling a story. You want ideas to resonate with an audience. Avoid presentations that look and feel like you are reciting a grocery list.

Want to Start on Third Base?
Try a (Better) Slide Template

While there is no out-of-the-box miracle template for slide decks, there is no harm in starting with something that a careful and creative designer has put together. A quick Google search will reveal some interesting places to start: many sites offer free templates that integrate well with Google Slides and PowerPoint and generally are possessed of a good (if somewhat conventional) design aesthetic. It is a challenge for many of us to find colors and fonts that work well together, not to mention creating design elements like arrows, bubbles, and myriad other icons—why not see what the talented, experienced folks have made for us? At least as a starting point, one could do worse.

CHAPTER 19

Defending Ideas

*Responding to Challenges, Extending
Your Thinking*

THE PREROGATIVE OF THE WRITER IS LUXURIOUS, VIEWED one way: the writer writes and then gives up some responsibility for the readers' ultimate view. We write, they read, and if they don't get it, well, we tried. But at the highest levels of scholarship that kind of freedom doesn't exist: you need not merely write your ideas but defend them to a live panel. Consider it an "essay *plus*"!

> **Remember:** Defending your ideas can be fun! Championships are more exciting than practices, and by this point in any academic project, you have earned the right to shine.

Nothing to fear, though: a defense isn't torture. It is an opportunity to reassert that you are an expert, that you have learned things, and that you have valuable things to say on the topic. By its nature, a defense is slightly adversarial, yes, but that's OK: scholarship is more like wrestling than dancing. After you present your findings—after you have done your best to make your case clear with a well-supported argument (and, in some cases, after you have designed a compelling slide design to advance a thoughtful set of ideas)—you get to be subjected to a few excellent questions to challenge you even further.

Why, god (?!), you might say. I've done enough! I've developed a meaningful question, I've performed the highest quality research I can, I've written a well-supported paper, and then presented my ideas in person: that should be sufficient! Yet, in academic circles, the most important part is the conversation afterwards: the defense. You wanted to join the academic conversation? Well, this is it.

I suggest that you try to find ways to enjoy it. Rarely will you enjoy the focus and attention you receive during a defense. Now you get to defend yourself: to answer the questions—usually sympathetic, though some may be tough—with grace, sincerity, and dexterity. You get to prove your critics wrong, or at least show them that your ideas can stand up to close scrutiny.

What Kinds of Questions Will You Be Asked?

In general, there are a few kinds of questions typically asked in any defense. This is true in our studies, and it will be remarkably similar if and when you defend a graduate thesis.

1. **Origins of the Research Question**
   Where did the question come from? What inspired it? How did the research question evolve as you conducted your research?

2. **Original Value of Your Work**

   How does your set of ideas advance the field? How do these ideas add to—or complexify—the ideas already out there on this topic? And how might your ideas shape the future research agenda of others? What are the implications of your work?

3. **Sources of Evidence**

   In any defense, discussing the reliability and credibility of the sources you used is of utmost importance. Your panel will want to hear that you have thought carefully about the value and limits of the evidence you used. Be prepared to discuss the evidence with clarity and specificity. Which sources were best? Why? What are the limits and gaps in your sources?

4. **Extending Your Research**

   Panelists generally expect you to know how your work shapes the future academic conversation on your topic. We want to see that you have considered how this work might lead to other work, too—what gaps still exist, and what sorts of new questions have emerged from this work. Based on what you learned in this research, what might you choose to study next?

How to Best Answer These Questions?

As always, we are haunted by the curse of knowledge: we know our research well, and when we go to discuss it, we often leave out important details, facts, and specifics. As always, we should be trying to get our audiences' brains to understand things as we do. If someone asks you to describe how you developed your research question, you need something more substantial than "It's just something I was interested in...." Why? What readings prompted it? Where did those readings take you? What did you find as you explored it? Why did this strike you as worthy of your attention?

You might be worried about droning on or boring your panelists—likely, the opposite will happen, and they will not really understand the depth of your thinking on this question. The curse of knowledge means that you will tend to assume the audience already knows things they don't and understands your ideas as well as you do. They need help to come to an understanding even close to the one you have. Be sure your answers to defense questions are thorough, that they account for the relative ignorance of your panelists, and that an-intelligent-but-uninformed observer will be guided to a meaningful understanding after listening to your response. When you think you are being detailed enough, come back to one or more of your simplest and most central points, and expand on those. When you think you've been too detailed and comprehensive, you're likely getting close to the right level of precision and clarity.

CHAPTER 20

Conversations about Research, Writing, and Presenting

Commonly Asked Questions

EACH OF THE FOLLOWING QUESTIONS HAS BEEN ASKED—OR implied—during my time teaching research, academic writing, and presentation skills. Consider this a composite of the most commonly asked questions.

I Can't Think of Any Research Questions. What Should I Do?

Read widely, listen to podcasts, and ask intelligent people you respect. Listen to ideas out in the world.

I Don't Have a Research Question, but My Topic Is Good. Why Do I Need a Research Question?

A general topic ("the economy," "climate change," etc.) is a kiss of death in academic work. If you begin with just a generic question, you will likely end up with little more than a jumbled collection of unconnected ideas. Your job as an academic writer is to focus on highly structured inquiry, not merely to recite a set of facts.

Invest heavily in the research question. It will guide your research, which will allow you to learn more, and therefore later write with greater depth, clarity, and subtlety. (Of course, the research question typically requires revision, too—once you start researching, you'll find you can ask better and better questions.)

Why Can't I Research Something That Is Happening Right Now?

The best evidence to answer any particular question typically requires years to gather. The most expert researchers require some time to produce the most thoughtful research papers, resting on the best evidence. You won't find the highest-quality evidence on something that just happened. For example, in the aftermath of the surprising Trump presidential victory in 2016, many students wanted to study it. But the only "evidence" available was speculation from pundits and newspapers. It would be years until thoughtful, evidence-based answers emerged from political scientists using voting and survey data.

Even more difficult is researching something that hasn't happened yet. It is possible, with the right kind of complex computer modeling, to produce tentative answers to the question: How bad will climate change be? But actually, most climate scientists are merely making decent guesses with models of staggering complexity. As an undergraduate, you will find that kind of original research impossible. Leave predictions to the psychics: stick to the things we can know with some confidence. Doing so means using the best sources available: peer-reviewed scholarship.

Remember: Many of the most interesting questions evade research. Just because something is a great conversation topic, doesn't mean it will work as a research question.

I Can't Find Any Sources that Prove My Thesis. Can You Help Me?

This kind of question is perfectly understandable, but it suggests a confusion about the entire research and writing process. You should not be determined to develop an argument or thesis statement on the basis of your previous knowledge and biases; instead, you should be open to having the thesis statement emerge from what you learned by researching. The goal of research is not to find things that prove what you already believe, but rather to develop new, richer, more credible and well-founded beliefs. There is never a circumstance where the problem of "not finding sources to prove my thesis" should emerge—you will develop an argument from whatever you've learned.

I Can't Find Any Research on the Topic I Want to Use. What Should I Do?

You will need to get creative with the search databases. Google's search algorithm in its Google Scholar product is nearly as intuitive as the basic Google search. It fills in missing details in your search and makes very useful guesses about what kinds of papers you might find relevant. Add Google Scholar to your search arsenal.

I Don't Need to Write an Outline. Why Bother?

You do need to write an outline. Please bother. Your work will be much better for it. Writing a good outline reduces the need for revision later. (You will still need to do lots of revision, but much less than if you had no plan in the first place.)

My Thesis Isn't Very Strong. Is It Ok If I Am on Both Sides of a Topic?

This is a wonderful question that demonstrates the value of research. When we learn more about most things, our views become more subtle and nuanced. Some of the best questions have delicate answers—not a simple binary of yes/no, on/off. Take, for example, a question we have touched on a lot in this book: income inequality. Reasonable people can disagree on this topic. Even if we conclude that reducing income inequality (a conclusion that would nearly certainly be supported by an honest reading of the evidence), we would likely also have to concede that numerous attempts to reduce inequality have been accompanied by unintended negative consequences, too. You don't want to be on both sides of the fence all the time, but you do want to be able to see questions from more than one side. You should be able to highlight the weaknesses in your own view—be a critic of your own ideas.

If you are open to the complexity of an issue, you *will* still have an argument. Even if you were to conclude, for example, that after surveying all the available literature on a topic, not enough data exists to answer it, that in itself is an argument.

Remember: In a world of polarized opinions, we often fall into a heightened need to "be right" about our views; this impulse can lead to needlessly strident thesis statements. Better to acknowledge complexity and nuance.

Why Do I Need to Follow Formal Academic Style? Why Not Just Write the Way It Sounds Good to Me?

Scholarly language is important not so that you can affect the style of an academic, but to make your ideas clear. Language is public. We share conventions partly based on tradition, partly based on how our brains process information. All of us need to do our part to ensure the collective set of ideas we all produce is understood by a wider audience.

My Reference List Just Has a Few Errors. What's the Big Deal?

Even small errors in your reference list are worth fixing. Remember: citations are part of the system that establishes and maintains standards of academic honesty; they are also part of the common language of scholars. We need to get them right. Even two or three small formatting issues in our reference list are regrettable.

You will that find some instructors care a lot about all the fine details of citation and attribution style and that others are quite lax. You can hope to get the lax ones and pay careful attention to the grading scheme on any university assignment sheets. Or, you can just get it right all the time, and in so doing, never worry at all.

I Revise as I Write. I Don't See Why
I Need to Edit Again Once I'm Finished

All writers require time to formally and deliberately revise their work. In the writing process, your brain is doing thousands of things at once, and we need to forgive it for making incomplete, sloppy, or otherwise unclear sentences, ideas that really don't flow well, or that just generally confuse the reader. This issue—the imperfect first draft—is true for every writer.

Effective revision is only possible once you have some distance from your own work. When you write, your brain assumes your writing is better than it is—again, we all do this—so if you give yourself a few days between writing and revising, your brain will see your writing clearly and more like your reader will.

I Can't Get the Whole Paper
on an Academic Database.
Why Is Only the Abstract Available on ProQuest?

This is an important question. You will find that sometimes you are interested in finding a paper, but when you locate it in the academic databases, you find only the abstract. All academic subscription packages include full-text papers, but not all papers will be available. See Chapter 8 for more on this.

If I Can Only Find the Abstract,
Can I Just Cite the Abstract?

I advise against citing a paper without having access to the whole text. Part of academic honesty is being devoted to finding the best and richest evidence, and if you only have the abstract, well, you can't really meet that standard.

If your intention is merely to make a passing reference to the findings of a study, and the abstract clearly states that finding, then it might be acceptable. For example, if you would like to cite a paper that found academic improvement of 16 per cent in schools that got rid of summer vacation, well, maybe you could cite a paper while having access to the abstract alone. But you might be missing very important material from the methods that would give you pause (what if the study involved only three students?).

Important Writers on Style

Who Has Come Before Us?

IN SOME WAYS, THERE IS LITTLE PLACE FOR YET ANOTHER
book on clear writing. There have been others before this and hopefully many others after. I am a devoted fan of style guides, though, and I'm not sure the genre is or will ever be complete.

No style guide would be honest without acknowledging by name a couple of those that have come before. There are many others that could fill a list here, but these two books, and their authors, are the best places to begin. If you read these two books, even by nipping in and out of them over the years when it feels like the job of writing clearly is a little hopeless, you will find what was once difficult and mysterious easier and more obvious—even if just a little.

Strunk and White, *The Elements of Style*

This famous book has two authors, William Strunk, a writing composition instructor at Cornell, and his student, E.B. White. Strunk, the lead author, would become famous long after he retired from the classroom because of White, who went on to be not just the author of books like *Charlotte's Web* and *Stuart Little*, but also a contributor to the *New Yorker* for many decades.

Strunk wrote what he called his "little book," a collection of rules for writing clear and concise writing, in 1918 (the first version was published in 1920). White was charmed, the book shaped him, and decades later (Strunk having died), he was asked to prepare a new edition. The result would shape writers of English the world over. Eighteen rules were all it took in the original, but it has been expanded a little since. Rule 13 in the original is my favorite ("omit needless words"), as it was for White. Strunk especially hated the empty and needless phrase "the fact that," a good rule that even the master White had trouble following:

> I suppose I have written the fact that a thousand times in the heat of composition, revised it out maybe five hundred times in the cool aftermath. To be batting only .500 this late in the season, to fail half the time to connect with this fat pitch, saddens me, for it seems a betrayal of the man who showed me how to swing at it and made the swinging seem worthwhile. (8)

White was one of the finest writers of his time. There were few who could match his clarity and power, even though his literary voice was often gentle. As a small sample: in 1943, at a time when it looked like democracy might plausibly vanish, E.B. White wrote this small piece that will haunt you if you let it:

> We received a letter from the Writers' War Board the other day asking for a statement on "The Meaning of Democracy." It presumably is our duty to comply with such a request, and it is certainly our pleasure.
>
> Surely the Board knows what democracy is. It is the line that forms on the right. It is the don't in don't shove. It

is the hole in the stuffed shirt through which the sawdust slowly trickles; it is the dent in the high hat. Democracy is the recurrent suspicion that more than half of the people are right more than half of the time. It is the feeling of privacy in the voting booths, the feeling of communion in the libraries, the feeling of vitality everywhere. Democracy is a letter to the editor. Democracy is the score at the beginning of the ninth. It is an idea which hasn't been disproved yet, a song the words of which have not gone bad. It's the mustard on the hot dog and the cream in the rationed coffee. Democracy is a request from a War Board, in the middle of a morning in the middle of a war, wanting to know what democracy is. ("Meaning of Democracy")

Graff and Birkenstein, *They Say/I Say: The Moves That Matter in Academic Writing*

There are many guides on the topic of academic writing, but few are as useful as Gerald Graff and Cathy Birkenstein's *They Say/I Say: The Moves That Matter in Academic Writing*. It has been very influential since its first publication in 2005 and has gone on to shape many undergraduate students' writing. One of its great strengths is its use of templates; these worked examples point the way with clarity and precision to exactly *how* to join the broader academic conversation. The authors write with the experience of decades of teaching university students, and they respond to the needs of emerging writers with admirable depth and empathy. It is brief, compelling, and useful; you might learn something new every time you open it.

An Editing Checklist

Double Checking the Basics

☐ Is my thesis rich and clear? Do I have an argument (and not just "this paper will explore ...")?

☐ Does each paragraph begin with a topic sentence?

☐ Are my ideas well supported by evidence? Are my ideas well-explained?

☐ Is each paragraph fully developed (not 2–3 sentences)?

☐ Do I cite every time I use a not commonly known fact?

☐ Do I reduce unnecessary direct quotations?

☐ Have I used enough high-quality sources (peer-reviewed especially)?

☐ Have I used plain but powerful vocabulary? Avoided needless personalization?

☐ Have I omitted needless words? Rule 13: http://www.bartleby.com/141/strunk5.html

☐ Have I generally avoided the passive voice?

☐ Have I considered various elements or dimensions of the question—and importantly, alternative views?

☐ Have I "put scholars in conversation with each other"?

☐ Have I demonstrated the credibility of my evidence? At least some key pieces of evidence?

- ☐ Do I extend my argument in the conclusion of my paper? Maybe by considering the implications or consequences of my argument?
- ☐ Have I avoided needless capitalization? (Capitalize only proper nouns.)
- ☐ It's = it is   Its = possessive?
- ☐ Have I avoided comma splices (joined independent clauses with a comma)?
- ☐ Is my entire paper double spaced?

APPENDIX C

Important Resources to Have at Hand

SOME MATERIAL OF GREAT IMPORTANCE IS BEST LEFT TO the internet. Please bookmark these sites, and organize them in a bookmarks folder in your browser for ease of access.

1. **A Good Writing Handbook / Reference Guide.** There are many good ones available. Among the best is *The Broadview Guide to Writing*, which has several authors; Graff and Birkenstein fairly describe it as "smart, helpful, and even fun to read"; even more important, it's generally very reliable. For years the most popular handbook was Diana Hacker's *A Writer's Reference* (which has been updated by others since her death in 2004); it remains among the leading choices. It's dry but it's comprehensive and it's almost always reliable on points of grammar and usage. None of the free online writing reference guides come close to either of these in comprehensiveness or reliability. The best of them is OWL Purdue (the Online Writing Lab from Purdue University), but it's not always to be trusted on matters of grammar and usage (it's more reliable on APA style ...)

2. **The Punctuation Guide.** There are literally thousands of punctuation guides online, but the best in my view is https://www.thepunctuationguide.com/. Keeping this guide close at hand is a very good idea.

3. **Your Library.** The modern, free, public library is truly one of the wonders of the modern world, and this library system is an example of why. Libraries demonstrate in their own quiet way the vital importance of so many things we care about: democracy, creativity, vitality, ideas, conversation, and nearly everything else of importance in civilized life.

4. **Academic Databases.** As mentioned in the text, Google Scholar (https://scholar.google.com/) is a very powerful academic search engine and should always be consulted, but beware: not all papers found here are open access. You can find them in Google Scholar, then perform a "full-text" search for them in ProQuest or EBSCO.

References
and Further Reading

"AP Seminar." *College Board*, 2022, apstudents.collegeboard.org/courses/ap-seminar.

Ballantyne, Nathan, and David Dunning. "Skeptics Say, 'Do Your Own Research.' It's Not That Simple." *New York Times*, 3 Jan. 2022,www.nytimes.com/2022/01/03/opinion/dyor-do-your-own-research.html.

Baretta, Luciane, et al. "Inference Making While Reading Narrative and Expository Texts: An ERP Study." *Psychology & Neuroscience*, vol. 2, no. 2, 2009, p. 137, psycnet.apa.org/fulltext/2011–14939–005.html.

"Canada on D-Day by the Numbers." *Juno Beach Centre*, 2020, www.junobeach.org/canada-on-d-day-by-the-numbers.

Didion, Joan. "Last words." *The New Yorker*, 9 Nov. 1998, www.newyorker.com/magazine/1998/11/09/last-words-6.

"Easy Reading Is Damned Hard Writing." *Quote Investigator*, 2020, quoteinvestigator.com/2014/11/05/hard-writing/.

"An Elephant in the Room." *Cambridge Dictionary*, dictionary.cambridge.org/dictionary/english/an-elephant-in-the-room.

Fadulu, Lola. "Study Shows Income Gap between Rich and Poor Keeps Growing, with Deadly Effects." *The New York Times*, 10 Sept. 2019, www.nytimes.com/2019/09/10/us/politics/gao-income-gap-rich-poor.html.

Gopnik, Adam. *Angels and Ages: A Short Book about Darwin, Lincoln, and Modern Life*. Vintage, 2010.

Graff, Gerald, and Cathy Birkenstein. *They Say/I Say: The Moves That Matter in Academic Writing*. Norton, 2014.

Hanauer, Nick, and David M. Rolf. "The Top 1% of Americans Have Taken $50 Trillion from the Bottom 90%—and That's Made the U.S. Less Secure." *Time Magazine*, 14 Sept. 2020, time.com/5888024/50-trillion-income-inequality-america/.

Heath, Chip, and Dan Heath. *Made to Stick: Why Some Ideas Survive and Others Die*. Random House, 2007.

Henville, Letitia. "Simple Tricks to Add Clarity in Complex Sentences." *University Affairs*, 14 Feb. 2020, www.universityaffairs.ca/career-advice/ask-dr-editor/simple-tricks-to-add-clarity-in-complex-sentences/.

Jiang, Suhang. "A Review of the Effectiveness of Gamification in Education." *SSRN*, 2016, papers.ssrn.com/sol3/papers.cfm?abstract_id=3163896.

Kahneman, Daniel, and Angus Deaton. "High Income Improves Evaluation of Life but Not Emotional Well-Being." *Proceedings of the National Academy of Sciences*, vol. 107, no. 38, 7 Sep. 2010, pp. 16489–93.

Kakwani, Nanak C. *Income Inequality and Poverty*. World Bank, 1980.

Kohan, Andrea, and Brian P. O'Connor. "Police Officer Job Satisfaction in Relation to Mood, Well-Being, and Alcohol Consumption." *The Journal of Psychology*, vol. 136, no. 3, May 2002, pp. 307–18. *ProQuest*, search.proquest.com/docview/213835897?accountid=36317.

Kolbert, Elizabeth. "The Psychology of Inequality." *The New Yorker*, 15 Jan. 2018, www.newyorker.com/magazine/2018/01/15/the-psychology-of-inequality.

Kopp, Carol M. "Income Inequality." *Investopedia*, 7 Nov. 2019, www.investopedia.com/terms/i/income-inequality.asp.

Kupferberg, Natalie, and Bridget McCrate Protus. "Accuracy and Completeness of Drug Information in Wikipedia: An Assessment." *Journal of the Medical Library Association: JMLA*, vol. 99, no. 4, Oct. 2011, pp. 310–13.

Kuznets, Simon. "Economic Growth and Income Inequality." *The American Economic Review*, vol. 45, no. 1, Mar. 1955, pp. 1–28.

Lee, Chelsea. "Title Case and Sentence Case Capitalization in APA Style." *APA Style Blog*, 9 Mar. 2012, blog.apastyle.org/apastyle/2012/03/title-case-and-sentence-case-capitalization-in-apa-style.html.

Lincoln, Abraham. "The Gettysburg Address." *Cornell University*, 2013, rmc.library.cornell.edu/gettysburg/good_cause/transcript.htm.

MacMillan, Margaret. *History's People: Personalities and the Past.* House of Anansi Press, 2015.

MLA Handbook. 9th edition. Modern Language Association, 2021.

Ophir, Eyal, et al. "Cognitive Control in Media Multitaskers." *Proceedings of the National Academy of Sciences*, vol. 106, no. 37, 2009, pp. 15583–87.

Penn, Jordan. *The Punctuation Guide*. www.thepunctuationguide.com/.

Piketty, Thomas. *Capital in the Twenty-First Century*. Translated by Arthur Goldhammer, The Belknap Press of Harvard UP, 2017.

Pinker, Steven. *The Better Angels of Our Nature: Why Violence Has Declined*. Penguin Group, 2012.

————. "One Thing to Change: Anecdotes Aren't Data." *The Harvard Gazette*, 21 June 2019, news.harvard.edu/gazette/story/2019/06/focal-point-harvard-professor-steven-pinker-says-the-truth-lies-in-the-data/.

————. *The Sense of Style: The Thinking Person's Guide to Writing in the 21st Century*. Penguin Books, 2015.

Poser, Bill. "Strunk and White vs. The Declaration of Independence." *Language Log*, 4 July 2006, itre.cis.upenn.edu/~myl/languagelog/archives/003318.html.

Rector, Lucy Holman. "Comparison of Wikipedia and Other Encyclopedias for Accuracy, Breadth, and Depth in Historical Articles." *Reference Services Review*, vol. 36, no. 1, 2008, pp. 7–22.

Ripley, Amanda, et al. "Room for Debate: How to Ensure Teacher Quality." *The New York Times*, 3 Mar. 2015, www.nytimes.com/roomfordebate/2015/03/03/how-to-ensure-and-improve-teacher-quality.

Rosalsky, Greg. "If a Wealth Tax Is Such a Good Idea, Why Did Europe Kill Theirs?" *NPR*, 26 Feb. 2019, www.npr.org/sections/money/2019/02/26/698057356/if-a-wealth-tax-is-such-a-good-idea-why-did-europe-kill-theirs.

Roser, Max, and Esteban Ortiz-Ospina. "Literacy." *Our World in Data*, 2016, ourworldindata.org/literacy.

Sagarra, Nuria, and Gabriela C. Zapata. "Blending Classroom Instruction with Online Homework: A Study of Student Perceptions of Computer-Assisted L2 Learning." *ReCALL*, vol. 20, no. 2, 2008, pp. 208–24.

Schleicher, Andreas. *PISA 2018: Insights and Interpretations*. OECD, 2019, www.oecd.org/pisa/PISA%202018%20Insights%20and%20Interpretations%20FINAL%20PDF.pdf.

Strunk, William, and E.B. White. *The Elements of Style*. W.P. Humphrey, 1918. *Bartleby.com*, revised, 1999, www.bartleby.com/141/.

Surowiecki, James. "The Cult of Overwork." *The New Yorker*, 19 Jan. 2014, www.newyorker.com/magazine/2014/01/27/the-cult-of-overwork.

White, E.B. "The Meaning of Democracy." *The New Yorker*, 3 July 1943, www.newyorker.com/books/double-take/e-b-white-on-the-meaning-of-democracy.

White, E.B., and William Strunk. *The Elements of Style*. 4th ed., Allyn and Bacon, 2000.

"World Bank Open Data." *The World Bank*, data.worldbank.org/.

Index

This book is made of paper from well-managed FSC® - certified forests, recycled materials, and other controlled sources.

MIX
Paper from
responsible sources
FSC® C103567

PERMANENT